# CUBA AND THE INDEPENDENCE WAR IN GUINEA-BISSAU AND CAPE VERDE

## AMONG THE TITLES IN THIS SERIES

EDITED AND INTRODUCED BY MARY-ALICE WATERS

**Revolution and the Road to Peace in Colombia**
*Fidel Castro (2025, 2023)*

**Che Guevara on Economics and Politics in the Transition to Socialism**
*Carlos Tablada (2024, 1998)*

**Our History Is Still Being Written**
*Armando Choy, Gustavo Chui, Moisés Sío Wong (2017, 2005)*

**Cuba and Angola: The War for Freedom**
*Harry Villegas (2017)*

**"It's the Poor Who Face the Savagery of the US 'Justice' System"**
*The Cuban Five talk about their lives within the US working class (2016)*

**Women in Cuba: The Making of a Revolution Within the Revolution**
*Vilma Espín, Asela de los Santos, Yolanda Ferrer (2012)*

**Capitalism and the Transformation of Africa**
*Mary-Alice Waters, Martín Koppel (2009)*

**Cuba and the Coming American Revolution**
*Jack Barnes (2007)*

**The First and Second Declarations of Havana**
*(2007)*

**Marianas in Combat**
*Teté Puebla (2003)*

**From the Escambray to the Congo**
*Víctor Dreke (2002)*

**Playa Girón/Bay of Pigs**
*Fidel Castro, José Ramón Fernández (2001)*

**Che Guevara Talks to Young People**
*(2000)*

**Making History**
*Interviews with four Cuban generals (1999)*

**How Far We Slaves Have Come!**
*Nelson Mandela, Fidel Castro (1991)*

# Cuba and the Independence War in Guinea-Bissau and Cape Verde

## THE FALL OF THE LAST COLONIAL EMPIRE IN AFRICA

VÍCTOR DREKE CRUZ
COMMANDER "MOJA"

*Pathfinder*
NEW YORK LONDON MONTREAL SYDNEY

Edited by Martín Koppel and Mary-Alice Waters



ISBN 978-1-60488-216-2
Library of Congress Control Number 2025948947
Manufactured in Canada

Second printing, 2026

**COVER DESIGN**: Toni Gorton

**COVER PHOTOS**:

**TOP**: Escambray Mountains, Cuba, January 1966. Amílcar Cabral, leader of African Party for the Independence of Guinea and Cape Verde (PAIGC), with Fidel Castro. After both took part in Tricontinental Conference in Havana, Castro spent three days with Cabral in that rural area showing him how the Cuban Revolution was transforming it. They discussed how the Cuban government could aid the liberation struggle against Portuguese colonial rule in Guinea-Bissau and Cape Verde.

**BOTTOM**: PAIGC and Cuban combatants in guerrilla base in Sambuia, Guinea-Bissau. In back row: PAIGC commander Joaquim Furtado (with rifle); Alfonso Pérez Morales, "Pina" (second from left), head of Cuban internationalists in the Northern Front. (*Courtesy of Alfonso Pérez Morales*)

**BACK COVER**: Amílcar Cabral (left) and Víctor Dreke, Conakry, Guinea, 1967. (*Courtesy of Víctor Dreke*)

**PATHFINDER**
pathfinderpress.com
Email: pathfinder@pathfinderpress.com

CONTENTS

## MAPS



## PHOTOS



## BOXES

# VÍCTOR DREKE CRUZ

FOR MORE THAN SIX DECADES, Víctor Emilio Dreke Cruz has been a participant and leader in Cuba's revolutionary movement, led by Fidel Castro. He was a combatant in the revolutionary war that overthrew the US-backed dictatorship of Fulgencio Batista in January 1959. In subsequent years he helped lead the battles that defeated US-sponsored counterrevolutionary bands in Cuba's Escambray Mountains and was an internationalist combatant in the Congo and Guinea-Bissau. He has shouldered many other leadership responsibilities in the Cuban government, armed forces, and Communist Party.

Born in 1937 in Sagua la Grande, in the former Las Villas province (today Villa Clara), Víctor Dreke began his revolutionary activity at age fifteen, when he joined street protests in March 1952 opposing Batista's military coup. In 1954 Dreke joined the Youth Movement of the Third Regional Workers Federation in Sagua, serving as student secretary. He was president of the Student Association in his high school and a member of the Guatemala Solidarity

Committee, which protested the US-organized overthrow of the government of Jacobo Arbenz in 1954.

In 1955 Dreke actively supported a strike by two hundred thousand sugar workers in Las Villas province. Strikers and their supporters took over most of Sagua and several other towns. He joined the July 26 Movement, led by Fidel Castro, soon after it was founded in June 1955 and became head of an action and sabotage cell in Sagua. In May 1957 he led a student strike against the Batista dictatorship.

After a March 13, 1957, assault on the presidential palace in Havana by a student-based organization called the Revolutionary Directorate, Dreke helped found a group in Sagua called the March 13 Movement, which included students, workers, and collaborators of the July 26 Movement. By the end of 1957 he had been forced underground by the dictatorship's repression. In early 1958 Dreke made his way to the Escambray Mountains of central Cuba, where he joined a guerrilla front initiated by the Revolutionary Directorate. In October 1958 those forces came under the command of the Rebel Army column headed by Ernesto Che Guevara. Since late 1956 the Rebel Army, under Fidel Castro's command, had been leading the July 26 Movement and the revolutionary war against the Batista tyranny from the Sierra Maestra mountains of eastern Cuba.

Dreke participated in numerous battles including the capture of the towns of Báez and Manicaragua, and was wounded in combat at Placetas. In the decisive battle that captured the city of Santa Clara, in late December 1958, he was second-in-command of the Ramón Pando Ferrer Commando Unit, which seized a garrison of the dictatorship's Rural Guard. He ended the war with the rank of captain in the Rebel Army.

Following the triumph of the revolution in January 1959, Dreke shouldered numerous responsibilities, including as a prosecutor for the revolutionary tribunals that put on trial many of the Batista regime's torturers and murderers.

In April 1961 he led two companies of the Revolutionary National Militias in the battle at Playa Girón, where the US-organized mercenary invasion at the Bay of Pigs was defeated. He was wounded in combat. In 1962 he was promoted to the rank of commander.

In 1962 special units known as Lucha Contra Bandidos (LCB, Fight Against Bandits) were created to crush dozens of US-backed counterrevolutionary bands. Based in Cuba's mountainous regions, the bandits were terrorizing peasant families in order to reimpose a government subservient to Washington and to both US and Cuban landlords and capitalists. Dreke was deputy commander of the LCB within the Central Army and headed its operations in the Escambray, where most of the bandits were concentrated. He led the ground units that by mid-1965 had wiped out or captured nearly all of them.

From April to November 1965 Dreke served as second in command, under Ernesto Che Guevara, of Cuban internationalist combatants in the Congo, which had won its independence from Belgium in 1960. The Cuban volunteers went there at the request of leaders of the Congolese national liberation movement who had been followers of Patrice Lumumba, leader of the Congo's independence fight who was assassinated in 1961. The Cubans helped train forces combating pro-imperialist troops and mercenaries in that country. In the Congo Guevara gave Dreke the nom de guerre Moja ("One" in Swahili). In Africa that is the name by which he has been known ever since.

Returning to Cuba he headed the Interior Ministry's Military Unit 1546, which trained internationalist volunteer combatants to aid national liberation struggles abroad. In 1967–68 he was sent back to Africa to head Cuba's military mission in both Guinea-Bissau and neighboring Guinea-Conakry. At that time Guinea-Bissau was fighting for its independence from Portugal—the subject of the firsthand account in these pages.

Dreke headed the group of Cuban military instructors fighting alongside the guerrillas of the African Party for the Independence of Guinea and Cape Verde (PAIGC). He also directed the Cuban volunteers who trained newly formed militias in the Republic of Guinea (also known as Guinea-Conakry) to help defend that country from imperialist threats. Guinea-Conakry served as the rear base for the PAIGC.

From 1986 to 1989 Dreke again served in Guinea-Bissau, this time as an adviser to the armed forces of that now-independent nation.

From 1965 to 1975 Dreke served as a member of the Central Committee of the Cuban Communist Party. In 1969 he was head of the Political Directorate of the Ministry of the Revolutionary Armed Forces. In 1973 he was named chief of the newly formed Youth Army of Labor (EJT) in Oriente province. Composed of young army recruits, the EJT worked in the countryside on some of the most difficult and challenging agricultural development projects.

Dreke graduated from the Máximo Gómez Military Academy of the Revolutionary Armed Forces (FAR) in 1972 with a degree in political science. In 1981 he graduated with a law degree from the University of Santiago de Cuba. He has received numerous decorations in Cuba as well as Africa, including the Order of Amílcar Cabral and the National Order of Colinas do Boé, conferred by the governments of Cape Verde and Guinea-Bissau, respectively.

In 1990 Víctor Dreke, holding the rank of colonel in the FAR, left active military service for the reserves. He was the representative in Africa for Cuban enterprises building housing, schools, roads, and other development projects. From 2003 to 2008 he served as Cuba's ambassador to Equatorial Guinea. On his return to Cuba he served for more than a decade as national vice president of the Association of Combatants of the Cuban Revolution and president of the association in Havana. He is currently president of the Cuba-Africa Friendship Association.

# Introduction

MARY-ALICE WATERS

*Cuba and the Independence War in Guinea-Bissau and Cape Verde: The Fall of the Last Colonial Empire in Africa* brings to life one of the most important chapters in the vast wave of anticolonial, anti-imperialist struggles that swept the globe during and in the aftermath of World War II.

It is a chapter rich in political lessons for the toilers. And a chapter that is also among the least known.

This is a firsthand account of that historic struggle by Víctor Dreke Cruz. As a young but already seasoned commander of Cuba's Revolutionary Armed Forces, in 1967–68 Dreke led Cuba's internationalist military mission in the West African countries of Guinea-Bissau and Guinea-Conakry.

Initiated by Cuban leaders Fidel Castro and Ernesto Che Guevara, the mission provided both military training and medical help to the cadres of the African Party for the Independence of Guinea and Cape Verde (PAIGC) led by Amílcar Cabral. The PAIGC combatants fought to put an end to five hundred years of Portuguese colonial exploitation and domination. The triumph of the Guinean people over that regime triggered the collapse of the last colonial empire in Africa, bringing independence not only for Guinea-Bissau in 1974 but, a year later, for Cape Verde, Angola, Mozambique, and São Tomé and Príncipe.

It also brought down the decayed fascist regime in Portugal itself.

Víctor Dreke's account of that turning point is not a dry "history." What comes to life in these pages is the pride and confidence of a previously subjugated and exploited people fighting not only for their own freedom but, as Cabral expressed it, coming to see themselves as part of "humanity's soldiers" and acting accordingly.

Alongside them you will also meet revolutionary Cuba's internationalist volunteers, who showed the world the kind of human solidarity that men and women transformed by making a genuine socialist revolution are capable of.

In the 1950s and 1960s a tsunami of anticolonial and anti-imperialist movements swept across Asia and the Pacific, Africa, the Middle East, and the Caribbean. It was a by-product of World War II itself. The second inter-imperialist slaughter of the twentieth century was waged by rival world powers for redivision and plunder of the earth's markets and natural resources. The deadliest war in human history, it ended an estimated seventy to eighty-five million lives. Most were civilians.

To understand the class character of that war, we must add that the overwhelming majority of those deaths, civilian and military alike, were of workers, peasants, small traders. The oppressed and exploited humanity of all races and nationalities.

From the ashes of World War II, US capitalism emerged as the dominant economic and military power. More important, the imperialist world order, born in the closing years of the nineteenth century, had been vastly weakened. In a few short years the colonial empires built (some over centuries) by Portugal, Spain, France, England, the Netherlands, Italy, Belgium, Germany, Japan, and the United States crumbled in face of victorious national liberation struggles the world over.

The relationship of forces on an international scale was changed.

The impact of that revolutionary upsurge reached inside the imperialist centers too. It inspired battles for rights, jobs, and human dignity by oppressed nationalities from Ireland and Quebec, to Australia, New Zealand, the Pacific Islands, and beyond.

Above all, the anticolonial movements in Africa helped fuel the historic battle that exploded in the United States itself, as working-class men and women who were Black, with growing confidence and pride, stood up to the most formidable imperialist ruling class on earth. Over a decade of increasingly powerful mobilizations, they brought down the entire capitalist structure of "Jim Crow" segregation that for three quarters of a century had dominated—and retarded—social relations across the North American continent. Their example, demonstrating what the working class in action is capable of achieving, brought to political life an entire generation of youth of all races. It opened the door to the racial integration of the modern labor movement and forever changed race and class relations throughout the United States.

This anti-imperialist and anticapitalist tide reached its highest political level with the opening of the Cuban Revolution on Washington's doorstep. The movement of Cuban working people forged under Fidel Castro's leadership toppled the US-backed Batista dictatorship in 1959 and opened the first socialist revolution in the Americas. For the US ruling class, that was a "crime" the owners of capital and their government will never forgive nor forget.

In 1960 alone, seventeen new African nations established their independence, and another fifteen did so before the end of the decade. By 1970 the only colonial empire still standing was the oldest: Portugal's.

How the Portuguese empire's underestimated subjects brought it down is the subject of this book.

Two things especially stand out in the account by Víctor Dreke, which is supplemented in the last chapter by the reflections of several other Cuban volunteers who also put their lives on the line in "Portuguese Guinea" or were part of leading that eight-year internationalist mission.

The first is the political importance and detailed attention Fidel Castro, Che Guevara, and other leaders of the Cuban Revolution gave to the national liberation struggles sweeping Africa. And the importance those struggles had for educating the people of Cuba about their own history and the realities of capitalist exploitation.

As Fidel often reiterated, the Cuban people's internationalist aid to those struggles was "paying our debt to humanity." Their course of action—from Algeria to the Congo, Guinea-Bissau, Ethiopia, Angola, and beyond—was not only an act of solidarity, however. It strengthened Cuban working people and their revolution as well.

The best known example is Cuba's contribution to defending the newly independent Angola from multiple invasions by apartheid South Africa. That internationalist mission spanned sixteen years, from 1975 to 1991. Its importance for all of Africa—and the world—was singled out by South African hero Nelson Mandela shortly after he was freed in 1990 after more than twenty-seven years in the prisons of the apartheid regime.

Speaking to a crowd of tens of thousands in Matanzas, Cuba, on July 26 that same year, Mandela thanked the Cuban people for their decisive aid, including the 425,000 volunteers who served in Angola, more than two thousand of whom gave their lives there. He underscored the "truly historic significance of their presence and reinforcement" in the 1988 battle of Cuito Cuanavale in southern Angola.

"The crushing defeat of the racist army at Cuito Cuanavale was a victory for the whole of Africa!" Mandela told the world. It has been "a turning point in the struggle to free the continent and our country from the scourge of apartheid."

Equally important was the impact inside Cuba of these internationalist missions. The hundreds of thousands of Cuban men and women who took part in one or more of Cuba's twenty-four missions in Africa over more than three decades came back as changed human beings. They had "broadened their scope," to use a favorite phrase of Malcolm X.

The generations of Cubans who were born and grew up after the triumph of the Cuban Revolution knew of capitalist exploitation only from books and the stories of their parents and grandparents. For them, living and fighting side by side with the people of Congo, Guinea-Bissau,

Ethiopia, Angola, and elsewhere was an unforgettable education in the barbarism of capitalism. It deepened their understanding of what Cuba's socialist revolution had accomplished, what it had opened.

Raúl Castro, then minister of the Revolutionary Armed Forces, expressed this in the clearest possible way in May 1991 as he welcomed home the last Cuban volunteer troops to leave Angola. Operation Carlota, as the Cuban military mission to Angola was named, was now completed, he said. And Raúl underscored its importance with these words:

"When we face new and unexpected challenges, we will always be able to recall the epic of Angola with gratitude. Because without Angola we would not be as strong as we are today," Raúl emphasized. "If our people know themselves better, if all of us know much better what we are capable of achieving," he said, "that, too, is thanks to Angola."

◆

The second thing that stands out in Víctor Dreke's account is the programmatic clarity, as well as the leadership capacities and conduct, of Amílcar Cabral, the central leader of the independence struggle in Guinea-Bissau and Cape Verde.

Cabral was assassinated in January 1973 in an operation organized by Portuguese intelligence forces. He didn't live to see the day in April 1974 when the eroded fascist regime in Portugal was overthrown by a military coup, a coup accelerated by spreading demoralization in the ranks and officer corps of the armed forces due to the defeats it was suffering in Guinea.

The PAIGC, and the liberation struggle its cadres led, survived Cabral's loss. More than anything, that was due to the fact that the political course Cabral led had won not only the support but the active participation of decisive numbers of Guineans and Cape Verdeans.

"We're not militarists," he insisted, addressing party cadres in 1966. "We're armed militants," political militants above all.

"Maybe I disappoint people, but I'm not a great defender of armed struggle," he told a US audience in 1972. "I am very conscious of the sacrifices demanded by armed struggle. It is violence even against our own people." If it "were possible to solve this problem without armed struggle, why not?" But a liberation war "is not our invention," he said. "It is the requirement of history."

Cabral had expressed himself even more simply and clearly when he spoke in 1966 to villagers who had joined the guerrilla army on the northern front of Guinean territory. "The armed struggle is very important, but the most important thing of all is an understanding of our people's situation," he told them.

"Our people support the armed struggle. We must assure them that those who bear arms are sons of the people and that arms are no better than the tools of labor," Cabral said. "Between one man carrying a gun and another carrying a tool, the more important of the two is the man with the tool. We've taken up arms to defeat the Portuguese, but the whole point of driving out the Portuguese is to defend the man with the tool."

Speaking in Dar es Salaam, Tanzania, at a 1965 conference of leaders of the liberation struggles in the Portuguese colonies, Cabral again explained the *political* cornerstone of the struggle in Guinea-Bissau and Cape Verde:

"We are not fighting simply to hoist a flag and to have a national anthem." We are fighting, he said, "so that our peoples may never more be exploited by imperialists, not only Europeans, not only people with white skins, because we do not confuse exploitation or exploiters with the color of men's skins.

"Who is this enemy who dominates us?" Cabral asked. "This enemy is not the Portuguese people, nor even Portugal itself." It's not even Portugal's fascist dictator, António Salazar, he said. "The enemy is Portuguese *colonialism*."

Portugal, Cabral emphasized, "is an economically backward country, in which about *50 percent* of the population is illiterate." The fact that Portugal was (and still is) a class-divided society meant that Portuguese soldiers captured by the PAIGC forces were often illiterate themselves.

Portuguese prisoners of war were not brutalized or humiliated by the liberation fighters but treated with dignity and respect. They sometimes mixed freely in the camps with the liberation forces, sharing in daily tasks such as collecting firewood and carrying water. They were turned over to the Red Cross when the opportunity arose, not to the Portuguese army. There is even a photo in this book of them playing a soccer match with each other!

The armed struggle for independence had been launched in 1963. It was begun only after the PAIGC had established—through experience since their clandestine founding in 1956, including bloody colonial repression of strikes and public protests—that they had no alternative.

In a country with no industry and virtually no working class, they decided they first needed to go into the bush, village by village, and win support among people of all tribes. That's what they did over the course of two years, at the same time organizing clandestine cells in the towns. They sent young cadres to work with the rural villagers and learn the conditions of their lives. They fought to counter tribal antagonisms the Portuguese fostered and took advantage of in order to sharpen divisions.

They organized schools for children and adults—illiteracy in Guinea-Bissau had been more than 99 percent. They established clinics, health brigades, militias, village administrative councils, and judicial structures. They drew women into these activities; they opened the door for women to lead. And much more that readers will discover in this account.

"We decided to mobilize the population in the bush," Cabral explained. "A lot of people think we came to this decision by applying the theories of Mao Zedong or whoever, but at the time we didn't even know who Mao Zedong was. The needs of our land led us to make this decision," Cabral said, "and our own missteps showed us the way."

Cabral's watchword guiding the PAIGC cadres was: "Hide nothing from the masses of our people. Tell no lies. Expose lies whenever they are told. Mask no difficulties, mistakes, failures. Claim no easy victories." The admonition conveys the same confidence in the exploited and oppressed as the spirit that guided the men and women of the Rebel Army in Cuba's Sierra Maestra mountains.

In September 1973, more than six months before the fall of the Portuguese regime, the PAIGC was strong enough to organize a national assembly of representatives from the administrative bodies of villages across the liberated territories. The delegates elected from these areas declared Guinea-Bissau an independent country. Even before formal independence had been recognized by Portugal, these liberated zones already covered two-thirds of the country.

It's evident from what Amílcar Cabral did and what he said that he was a conscious materialist, a dialectical, historical materialist. He was comfortable with and had internalized what he had read of Marx and Engels. In a country still marked in many regions by pre-class social relations, Cabral understood and explained in a clear and simple way to audiences of all kinds that the history and evolution of humanity is based on the development of productive forces. History doesn't begin with the birth of class divisions and oppression. The social and economic antagonisms of capitalist society are therefore not eternal, but can be transformed by revolutionary action of the toilers.

Cabral urged young people, irrespective of religious convictions, to study science, to overcome traditional fears of nature. To study and learn from contact with other societies. He insisted that, whatever the similarities among national liberation struggles, the leaderships of each one must begin by understanding the uniqueness of the history and economic development of their people.

To those who condemned all things Portuguese, Cabral explained that capitalism in Europe and worldwide had played a huge and irreplaceable role in the evolution of human society and improvement of people's lives. Capitalism had once been the most productive force on earth. But that had changed fundamentally with the dawn of the imperialist epoch.

"While we get rid of colonial culture and negative aspects of our own culture," Cabral told the people of Guinea-Bissau and Cape Verde, "we have to create a new culture, also based on our traditions, but respecting everything that the world today has conquered for the service of mankind."

A person's "patriotism or sincerity cannot be measured by the color of their skin, their name, or the way they dress," Cabral explained. "Some among us think that if their name is N'Tan Passa, Keita, or Bubacar, or whatever, then for that reason alone they're more Guinean than someone called Lourenço Marques or Lúcio Vieira, which are white names. This isn't true. A name doesn't make someone more of a child of their land, more entitled to the land, more a friend of the people.

"A person's name or the color of their skin isn't what matters. What matters is what that person has in his head and in his heart. It's the work he does each and every day that makes him a true child of the land."

Speaking with a group of Black rights fighters during an October 1972 trip to the United States, Cabral answered a question by an American supporter about the status of women. "Yes, we have made great achievements, but not enough," he answered. "We are very far from what we want to do. But this is not a problem that can be solved by Cabral signing a decree. It is all part of the process of changing the material conditions of our people."

Cabral also responded to a question on Pan-Africanism during that US trip. "Pan-Africanism is a very nice idea, but we have to work for it," he said. He reminded his audience that in many newly independent African countries, "they only replaced a white man for a black man, but for the people it's the same." In an earlier speech he explained, "We are for African unity in favor of the African peoples. We consider unity to be a means, not an end. [It] must not betray the end. That is why we are not in such a great hurry to achieve African unity."

Speaking at the 1965 Dar es Salaam conference of liberation movements in the Portuguese colonies, Cabral emphasized that "our armed struggle is only one aspect of the general struggle of the oppressed peoples against imperialism, of man's struggle for dignity, freedom, and progress. In the vast front of struggle in Africa today, we should consider ourselves as soldiers, often anonymous, but soldiers of humanity."

Given the materialist foundation and class clarity guiding Cabral's political course, it is no surprise he was sometimes asked if he was a Marxist. His reply to such a question at a 1971 public meeting in London is a pleasure to read.

"Is Marxism a religion?" Cabral asked the questioner. "I am a freedom fighter in my country. You must judge from what I do in practice. If you decide it's Marxism, tell everyone it's Marxism. If you decide it's not Marxism, tell them it's not Marxism. But the labels are your affair; we don't like those kinds of labels.

"People here are very preoccupied with the questions: are you Marxist or not Marxist?," he added. "Please, just ask me whether we are doing well in the field. Are we really liberating our people, the human beings in our country, from all forms of oppression?

"Ask me simply this, and draw your own conclusions."

Cabral not only welcomed the internationalist aid the liberation movement received from the government and people of Cuba. He was attracted to the political example of the Cuban Revolution and its leadership.

"If any of us came to Cuba with doubts in our mind about the deep-rooted character, strength, maturity, and vitality of the Cuban Revolution," Cabral said in a speech in Havana in January 1966, "such doubts were dispelled by what we have already been able to see." He was presenting one of the keynote talks at the Tricontinental Conference, which had attracted some five hundred delegates from more than eighty countries around the world.

"The vanguard of the Cuban Revolution has mobilized, organized, and politically educated the people," Cabral continued. It has "kept them permanently informed about national and international questions that affect their lives," enabling them "to take an active part in addressing those problems.

"This constitutes a lesson for us, especially for the national liberation movements, and specifically for those who want their national revolution to be a true revolution."

As shown by these few examples and by others throughout Víctor Dreke's account, what marked the character and political course of Amílcar Cabral's leadership of the PAIGC was confidence in the revolutionary capacities of the exploited and oppressed. No wonder Fidel and Che recognized in Cabral a kindred soul and sent some of the best and most experienced cadres of the Cuban Revolution to aid them. To fight *alongside* them, as Cabral insisted, not *for* them.

Over the eight years of the war for independence, some four hundred Cuban internationalist volunteers at one time or another fought at the side of the liberation forces of Guinea and Cape Verde. They lived to the fullest Fidel's call to action:

"Those not willing to fight for the freedom of others will never be able to fight for their own."

SEPTEMBER 30, 2025

**"Hide nothing from the masses of our people. Tell no lies. Mask no difficulties, mistakes, failures. Claim no easy victories."** —AMÍLCAR CABRAL, 1965

COURTESY OF VÍCTOR DREKE

Amílcar Cabral knew the liberation movement in Guinea-Bissau and Cape Verde could only be successful by winning the support and active participation of the masses of people. The goal, he said, was "not simply to hoist a flag and have a national anthem"—formal independence—but to begin to transform society in the interests of the majority.

**ABOVE:** Cabral speaking to PAIGC fighters, women militia members, and local residents at the party's 1964 congress, held in the village of Cassacá. There he led a successful political battle against several guerrilla commanders who had become local warlords and were using their military authority to abuse women and terrorize the population.

# AFRICA

MOROCCO
TUNISIA
ALGERIA
LIBYA
EGYPT
WESTERN SAHARA
CAPE VERDE
MAURITANIA
MALI
NIGER
CHAD
SUDAN
ERITREA
SENEGAL
GAMBIA
BURKINA FASO
DJIBOUTI
NIGERIA
GUINEA-BISSAU
GHANA
CENTRAL AFRICAN REPUBLIC
SOUTH SUDAN
ETHIOPIA
CAMEROON
BENIN
SOMALIA
GUINEA-CONAKRY
TOGO
UGANDA
CÔTE D'IVOIRE
GABON
KENYA
SÃO TOMÉ & PRÍNCIPE
DEM. REP. OF CONGO (ZAIRE)
SIERRA LEONE
RWANDA
BURUNDI
TANZANIA
LIBERIA
EQUATORIAL GUINEA
MALAWI
ANGOLA
ZAMBIA
MOZAMBIQUE
CONGO-BRAZZAVILLE
NAMIBIA
ZIMBABWE
BOTSWANA
MADAGASCAR
Atlantic Ocean
SOUTH AFRICA
ESWATINI
LESOTHO
N
W
E
S
0 500 1000 miles
0 800 1600 kilometers

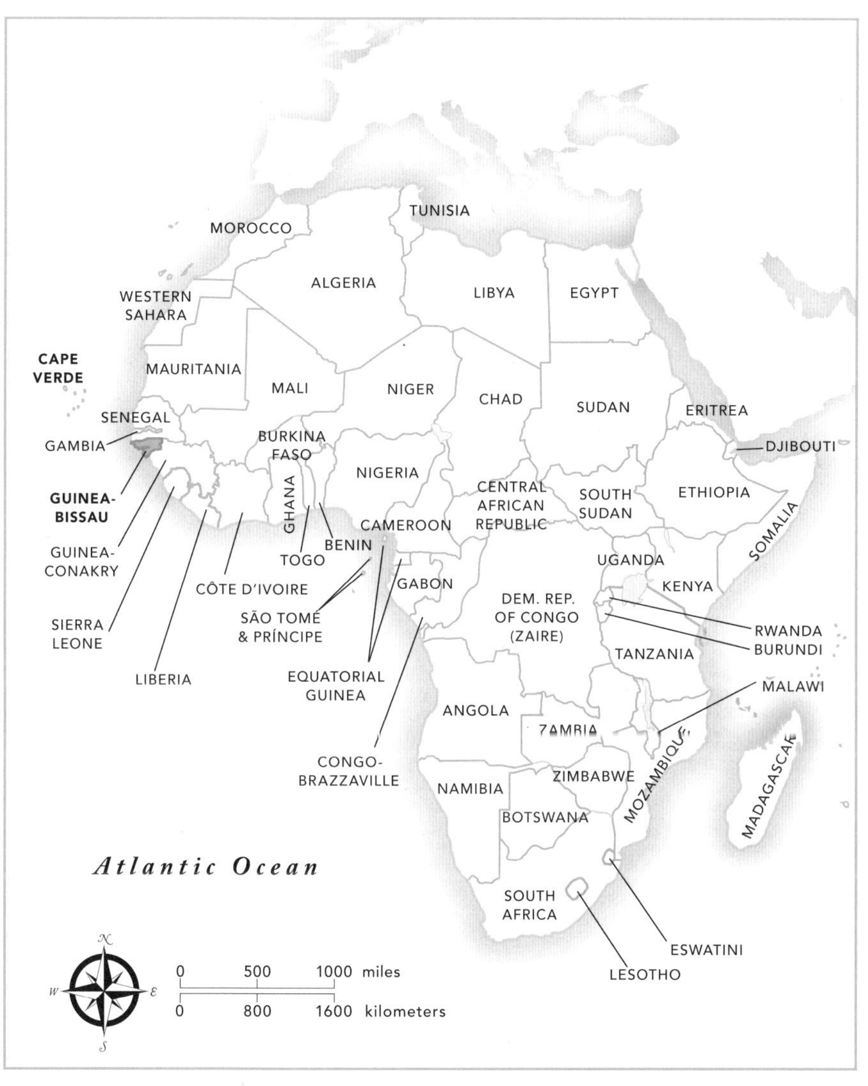

# WEST AFRICA

Atlantic Ocean
MOROCCO
TUNISIA
ALGERIA
LIBYA
WESTERN
SAHARA
MAURITANIA
CAPE
VERDE
MALI
NIGER
Praia
Dakar
SENEGAL
GAMBIA
Bissau
BURKINA
FASO
GUINEA-
BISSAU
BENIN
NIGERIA
Conakry
CÔTE
D'IVOIRE
GHANA
TOGO
GUINEA-
CONAKRY
SIERRA
LEONE
LIBERIA
CAMEROON
EQUATORIAL GUINEA
SÃO TOMÉ & PRÍNCIPE
GABON
0
500 miles
0
800 kilometers
CONGO-
BRAZZAVILLE

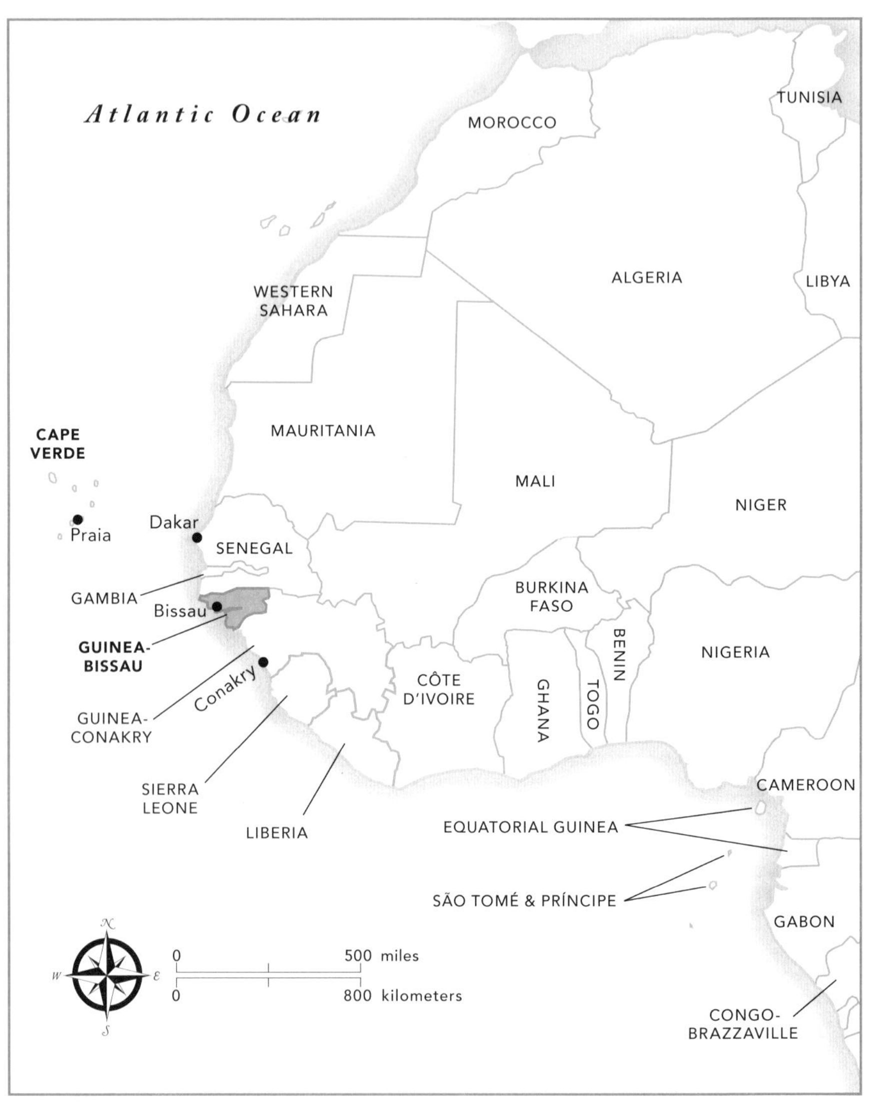

# GUINEA-BISSAU and CAPE VERDE

# Some background

MARTÍN KOPPEL

# Guinea-Bissau and Cape Verde

THE REPUBLIC OF GUINEA-BISSAU, in West Africa, is one of the smallest countries on that continent. With a territory of fourteen thousand square miles, roughly the size of Belgium, it has a population today of two million. The country's name is identified by its capital city, Bissau, to distinguish it from the neighboring Republic of Guinea, often called Guinea-Conakry, after its capital.

Portuguese is the official language of Guinea-Bissau, and an indigenous creole is widely spoken nationwide. The population also speaks languages corresponding to their respective ethnic groups, which include the Balanta, Fula (Fulani), Manjaco, Mandinga (Malinke), Pepel, and Bijagó peoples. Tribal and language ties straddle the borders with neighboring Senegal and Guinea-Conakry. Nearly half the population identifies as Muslim, especially among the Fulas and Mandingas. Significant numbers, particularly among the Balantas, Pepels, Manjacos, and Bijagós, practice animist religions or Catholicism.

For five centuries Guinea-Bissau was part of Portugal's colonial empire in Africa—along with Angola, Mozambique,

Cape Verde, and São Tomé and Príncipe. Lisbon used the Guinean coast as a center for its transatlantic slave trade. Many Africans were forced into slave labor on Portuguese cotton and indigo plantations in Cape Verde, an island chain 350 miles off the African mainland. Until the late nineteenth century the colonial rulers had little presence in the interior of what is now Guinea-Bissau; only by 1936 did they succeed in crushing indigenous resistance.

From 1933 to 1974 Guinea-Bissau was under the heel of the clerical-fascist dictatorship in Portugal headed by António Salazar and then by Marcelo Caetano. Lisbon kept its colonies largely isolated from the rest of the world. By the time Guinea-Bissau gained independence, it had virtually no industry, little infrastructure, and an overwhelmingly agricultural population. Only a small percentage of the arable land was cultivated, mostly rice for subsistence and peanuts as a cash crop.

Under Portuguese colonial law Guineans were divided into two categories: "assimilated" and "nonassimilated" (or "civilized" and "native"). A tiny number—less than one percent—who met certain literacy and tax requirements were recognized as "assimilated," which gave them access to public education and very limited political rights. The colonial rulers sought to convince them to identify as "Portuguese," even though they were barely third-class citizens.

More than 99 percent of the population was disenfranchised. Peasants in particular were subjected to innumerable taxes, forced labor on road construction, floggings, and theft of their livestock. In the 1950s Portuguese Guinea had one public high school. Literacy was less than 1 percent. The country had only twenty-five trained doctors and twenty-six nurses. Malaria, hookworm, sleeping sickness, river blindness, and other parasitic diseases were endemic. Malnutrition as well as high infant and maternal mortality rates were daily realities. Average life expectancy was thirty-seven.

Before independence, economic relations in the countryside were largely precapitalist. Social relations varied greatly between tribal groups. The Balantas were a preclass society, with land held communally and no social stratification; decisions were made by a council of elders in consultation with the villagers.

On the other hand, among the Fulas a hierarchical class structure had begun to emerge: chiefs, nobles, religious figures, artisans, itinerant traders, and peasants. According to tradition, Fula land belonged to the entire village and the chief's responsibility was to supervise land use in the interests of the community. In reality, Fula peasants were subject to the chiefs, to whom they had to turn over a portion of their agricultural produce. Other tribes were at stages of development somewhere between those of the Balantas and the Fulas.

The status of women also varied according to the economic and social relations in each tribal group. Among Balantas, women enjoyed a large degree of equality with men. In Fula communities, women were considered the property of men. Polygamy was widespread throughout the territory, although monogamy was more prevalent in Balanta communities. Women did most of the agricultural work among all tribal groups.

The Portuguese colonial regime used tribal, ethnic, religious, and other differences to try to keep the Guinean population divided, as well as to pit Guineans against Cape Verdeans. For example, during the independence war it gained cooperation from many of the traditional Fula chiefs by promising to protect their privileges. The African Party for the Independence of Guinea and Cape Verde (PAIGC) under the leadership of Amílcar Cabral combated the regime's divide-and-rule methods and won the support of the large majority of Guineans from all ethnic backgrounds.

### Cape Verde

Cape Verde is a chain of ten volcanic islands 350 miles off the coast of West Africa. It was uninhabited until the fifteenth century, when the Portuguese arrived and began to populate it with Africans captured and transported from the mainland.

Slavery dominated the islands' colonial economy until the nineteenth century. As a result of this history, most Cape Verdeans are *mestiços*, of mixed African and European descent, and a majority are Catholic. The official language is Portuguese, but people mostly speak *crioulo*, the Cape Verdean creole. The country today has more than five hundred thousand inhabitants, a third of whom live in the capital, Praia.

The colonial rulers classified Cape Verdeans as "assimilated," seeking to pit them against the majority in Guinea-Bissau. Cape Verdeans were given more access to public education and appointed to many civil service and low-level administrative jobs in the colonial regime.

Even so, in an arid country with little agricultural development, Cape Verdeans faced high unemployment, illiteracy, reliance on imports for most food, and catastrophic droughts and famines. Peasants, sharecroppers, and tenant farmers were exploited by large landowners. These conditions have led to massive emigration since the nineteenth century, including by those who under colonial rule were driven to find work as indentured laborers on the cacao plantations of São Tomé and Príncipe. Today more people of Cape Verdean ancestry live abroad than at home, with significant numbers in the United States, Senegal, Argentina, and Portugal and elsewhere in Europe.

During and after the second imperialist world war, national liberation movements exploded across Asia, Africa, and Latin America and the Caribbean. In the late 1950s and early '60s, most African countries freed themselves from British, French, Belgian, and Spanish colonial rule. The Portuguese colonies finally won their independence in the mid-1970s.

Amílcar Cabral was the central leader of the joint struggle in Guinea-Bissau and Cape Verde. They have had separate governments since winning their independence.

# Amílcar Cabral

AMÍLCAR CABRAL WAS BORN IN 1924 of Cape Verdean parents in Portuguese Guinea (today Guinea-Bissau) and grew up in Cape Verde.

After completing high school Cabral received a scholarship to attend the Technical University of Lisbon. He chose to study agronomy, with a special interest in soil science, because he wanted to find the root causes of the drought-induced famines that afflicted Cape Verde. He became convinced these were not inevitable natural disasters but the product of profit-driven deforestation and overgrazing under colonial rule—and could be prevented. His experiences and studies led him increasingly to become grounded in a scientific understanding of how human labor transforms nature and is the driving force of society's progress.

In Lisbon Cabral met fellow African students, including Agostinho Neto and Mário de Andrade from Angola, as well as Eduardo Mondlane and Marcelino dos Santos from Mozambique, who later became founding leaders of independence movements in their own countries; dos Santos and Cabral were even roommates for a while.

They became involved in political activity in Portugal with opponents of Salazar's fascist dictatorship, including the Communist Party. At that time, however, the pro-Moscow party, in order to facilitate its collaboration with "progressive" bourgeois allies, refused to champion independence for Portugal's colonies, just as the French Communist Party did not support the Algerian independence struggle. So the radicalizing African youth began to organize their own clandestine meetings on politics and culture, first at the House of Students of the Empire, a social center established by the Portuguese government, and then the Center for African Studies, which Cabral helped found. They frequented a social center for African sailors, who gave them prohibited books from abroad and helped them expand their political horizons.

Cabral spent some time working at an agricultural research station in rural Alentejo, the poorest region of Portugal, where he witnessed the exploitation, illiteracy, and landlord repression facing large numbers of landless peasants and *jornaleiros* (day laborers). That experience had a deep impact on Cabral. It helped awaken him to the understanding that working people in Portugal had common interests with those fighting imperialist rule in Africa and could be won to that struggle.

Returning to Portuguese-ruled Guinea in 1952, Cabral worked as an agronomist—the first in his country—and crisscrossed the territory to conduct a detailed agricultural census that was unprecedented in Portugal's African colonies. The year-long effort allowed him to meet hundreds of villagers and peasants and gain intimate knowledge about the land, economy, and peoples of Guinea-Bissau. He learned about the conditions they faced under the colonial boot—and the potential for transforming those conditions.

Cabral became a target of the Portuguese authorities in Bissau for encouraging "subversive" discussions in a youth sports club he organized. They banned him from the colony except for brief family visits, and he returned to Portugal. He also worked as an agronomist in Angola on several occasions, and joined in founding the Popular Movement for the Liberation of Angola (MPLA), led by his friend and comrade Agostinho Neto.

In September 1956 Cabral returned to Bissau, where he secretly founded the African Party for the Independence of Guinea and Cape Verde together with his brother Luís Cabral, Aristides Pereira, and other anticolonial fighters. Members of the young PAIGC led numerous struggles by working people.

A turning point was the 1959 strike in Bissau by dockworkers and riverboat sailors fighting miserable wages and job conditions. On August 3, 1959, Portuguese troops opened fire on the strikers at the Pidjiguiti docks, killing fifty. The Pidjiguiti massacre, today commemorated as a national holiday, convinced the PAIGC leadership that legal avenues of struggle were closed. They would have to wage a guerrilla struggle. The organization established its rear base in neighboring Guinea-Conakry, with the support of the government of President Ahmed Sékou Touré.

Over the course of two years prior to launching a guerrilla war in 1963, the PAIGC sent its young cadres to rural villages across Guinea-Bissau to learn from and win the confidence of the population. They recruited from all tribal groups.

At the first party congress, held in 1964 in the southern village of Cassacá, Cabral led a successful political battle to defeat several guerrilla commanders who had become local warlords. These officers had used their military authority to abuse women, accuse critics of "witchcraft" and kill them, and terrorize the population. The PAIGC was reorganized so the war would be led politically and militarily by the party's central leadership.

The movement made rapid advances against the colonial regime, establishing liberated zones in growing parts of Guinea-Bissau. In those areas the PAIGC organized the population to address basic social needs. They set up dozens of schools. Clinics treated patients without charge, and health brigades carried out vaccination campaigns against cholera. They established stores where peasants could obtain basic goods. Self-defense militias, together with the guerrilla army, protected villagers from Portuguese attacks. Elected village committees administered local affairs, and a judicial system was established. The PAIGC also organized an underground movement in the capital city of Bissau.

With Cabral's active encouragement, women were increasingly organized into social and political activity, becoming teachers, nurses, village committee members, political leaders, and combatants. Through these experiences growing numbers of women gained self-confidence, and age-old prejudices began to break down. The PAIGC leadership carried out educational work to end the bride-price and forced marriages, as well as to advocate a woman's right to divorce. It prohibited polygamy for its members, while seeking to persuade the broader population to oppose that practice.

Beginning in May 1966, at Cabral's request Cuba's revolutionary government sent internationalist volunteers to Guinea-Bissau who trained and fought alongside the independence fighters. Víctor Dreke led the Cuban units that served there in 1967–68.

In January 1973 Amílcar Cabral was assassinated in an operation organized by the Portuguese secret police and carried out by disaffected PAIGC members and former members. Exploiting ethnic antagonisms long fostered under colonial rule, the regime had recruited a number of Guineans who had personal grievances against the PAIGC leadership and were hostile to Cape Verdeans. Lisbon promised to reward them with high positions in a future "autonomous" Guinea-Bissau, in exchange for killing Cabral and ending "Cape Verdean domination" of the liberation movement.

Despite this hard blow, the independence movement continued advancing. With the support of the Cuban internationalists, the PAIGC dealt decisive defeats to the Portuguese army, which suffered increasing desertions. The liberation struggle in Guinea-Bissau detonated a political crisis in the decaying fascist regime in Lisbon, which was also waging colonial wars in Angola and Mozambique.

In April 1974 the Caetano dictatorship was overthrown in a military coup, sparking a mass popular upsurge in Portugal known as the "Carnation Revolution."

Guinea-Bissau won its independence in September 1974. Cape Verde became independent in 1975, as did Mozambique, Angola, and São Tomé and Príncipe.

# Interview with Víctor Dreke Cruz

The following is a firsthand account by Víctor Dreke Cruz of the events that led to the historic fall of the last colonial empire in Africa.

Dreke's account is the product of interviews conducted with the Cuban revolutionary leader over nearly two decades by Mary-Alice Waters, a leader of the Socialist Workers Party in the United States and president of Pathfinder Press, together with Pathfinder staff editors Martín Koppel and Róger Calero. They were aided by Iraida Aguirrechu, senior editor of Editora Política, then the publishing house of the Cuban Communist Party.

As explained earlier, Dreke's involvement in Guinea-Bissau's struggle for independence began in the mid-1960s—when the Cuban government responded to the African independence leaders' request for assistance—and continued after the people of Guinea-Bissau and Cape Verde freed themselves from colonial rule.

# 1. Why we went

**MARY-ALICE WATERS:** In November 1965 you returned to Cuba from the Congo,* where you had served as second-in-command under Ernesto Che Guevara of a column of 130 Cuban volunteers aiding anti-imperialist fighters there. Your account of that internationalist mission is the final chapter of the book we worked on together more than twenty years ago, *From the Escambray to the Congo: In the Whirlwind of the Cuban Revolution.*

Barely a year after your return, Fidel called on you to lead a new internationalist effort in Africa, this time as head of Cuba's military mission in Guinea-Bissau and in the neighboring Republic of Guinea, or Guinea-Conakry, as it's known.

The Cuban Revolution's contribution to the victorious war against Portuguese colonial rule in Guinea-Bissau was decisive, but it's not as widely known as the Congo mission you were part of. Many historical accounts of the lib-

* The Democratic Republic of the Congo (sometimes known as Zaire). It neighbors the Republic of the Congo. To distinguish the two countries, the former is referred to here as the Congo and the latter as Congo-Brazzaville, after its capital city.

eration movement in Guinea-Bissau and Cape Verde today don't even mention Cuba's support to that independence war. What can you tell us about it? Why did Cubans join the struggle there?

**VÍCTOR DREKE:** First let me start with a broader picture. Guinea-Bissau and the Cape Verde Islands were colonized by Portugal for five centuries, along with Angola, Mozambique, and São Tomé and Príncipe. The people of those territories were among the millions of Africans who were forcibly taken to the Americas as slaves, including many to Cuba.

In the 1950s and '60s, national liberation movements around the world fought colonial and imperialist domination. In Africa, most countries won their independence from British, French, Belgian, and Spanish rule, and liberation movements also arose in Portugal's colonies.

The African Party for the Independence of Guinea and Cape Verde, the PAIGC, was founded by Amílcar Cabral in 1956. It led and took part in struggles that were savagely repressed by the Portuguese regime. In 1959 the leaders of the movement concluded they would have to fight arms in hand as well as politically. In 1963 they launched a war for independence.

Why did we go to Guinea-Bissau? The Cuban Revolution has been internationalist from the start. Our first missions abroad were in Africa. In 1961, when the Algerians were fighting to free themselves from French colonial rule, the Cuban government sent them a shipment of weapons, and the ship brought back war orphans to receive medical treatment here in Cuba. The year after they won independence in 1962, we sent volunteer combatants to help Algeria defend itself from a US-instigated attack by the Moroccan regime. That same year Cuba's first group of internationalist doctors and nurses went to Algeria.

In December 1964 Che traveled to Africa to meet with governments and leaders of liberation movements throughout the continent. That trip, which lasted three months, led to the decision by our revolutionary leadership in 1965 to send a column of Cuban combatants to the Congo, headed by Che. We went at the request of Congolese who were fighting a neocolonial regime, and with the official backing of the Organization of African Unity, the association of the newly independent African countries. We served as instructors and fought alongside the Congolese combatants.

During his earlier trip to Africa Che visited Guinea-Conakry. There he met Amílcar Cabral and was impressed with his qualities as a leader. Che concluded that the movement in Guinea-Bissau was one of the most serious and best organized in Africa.

Just a few months later Cuba fulfilled a pledge Che had made to Amílcar. We sent a ship, the *Uvero*, with arms, medicine, and food for the guerrilla fighters in Guinea-Bissau. It was unloaded in Guinea-Conakry, which under President Ahmed Sékou Touré was providing a rear base for the PAIGC.

**WATERS:** In January 1966, Cabral was in Havana for the Conference of Solidarity with the Peoples of Asia, Africa, and Latin America—the Tricontinental Conference—which brought together anti-imperialist fighters from around the world. In his speech to that gathering, Cabral paid tribute to Cuba's socialist revolution.

**DREKE:** Amílcar gave a serious speech, the best speech at the Tricontinental Conference.* He explained that armed

---

* See excerpts on pp. 54–55.

struggle was necessary in national liberation struggles like the one they were waging against Portuguese colonialism. At that time, left-wing organizations in many countries were advocating a "peaceful road" in the fight against imperialist domination. And here was Amílcar embracing the Cuban Revolution and Fidel on the need for revolutionary armed struggle.

After the conference Fidel took Cabral to the Escambray Mountains for three days. He showed him how the revolution had transformed the living conditions of the peasants, and how we had defeated the US-backed counterrevolutionary bandits in the Escambray.

Amílcar told Fidel about the fight they were waging against Portuguese colonialism, the advances they were making, and the difficulties they faced.

Right away, Fidel understood the challenges Cabral was describing. Fidel pledged that Cuba would send them artillery instructors and doctors. The guerrilla fighters also lacked transportation, so he promised trucks and mechanics. The first group of Cubans arrived in Guinea-Bissau in mid-1966.

Fidel's assessment, like Che's, was that if there was a liberation movement in Africa with real potential for victory, it was the PAIGC. And that a victory in Guinea-Bissau would give a big impetus to the struggles in the other Portuguese colonies, Angola and Mozambique.

**WATERS:** Cabral was highly regarded among anti-imperialist fighters throughout Africa.

**DREKE:** Amílcar was respected not only by the people of Guinea-Bissau and Cape Verde, but by liberation movements across the continent.

For example, he went to Congo-Brazzaville in 1966 for a meeting of leaders of the Conference of Nationalist Organizations in the Portuguese Colonies, which included Angola, Mozambique, and Guinea-Bissau. They visited a camp where Cuban instructors were training combatants of the MPLA, the Popular Movement for the Liberation of Angola. A ceremony was held there, and Amílcar was chosen to give the speech on behalf of the entire delegation. In that speech he gave special thanks to the Cuban internationalists for their solidarity.*

**MARTÍN KOPPEL:** What was Cabral's background?

**DREKE:** Amílcar was born in Bafatá, the second-largest city in Guinea-Bissau, and he grew up in Cape Verde. He received a university scholarship to study in Portugal and graduated with a degree in agronomy. The Portuguese authorities were hoping to prepare him to become an exploiter of his own people, as they had done with other leaders in their colonies. Amílcar ended up with an education. But he didn't sell out.

He became the first African agricultural engineer—not just in Guinea-Bissau, but in Africa. And he used his scientific and technical knowledge to become completely acquainted with the economic, social, and geographic conditions in his country.

While he was at the university in Lisbon he became involved in political activities with other African students.

**WATERS:** Crispina Gomes, the Cape Verdean ambassador here in Cuba, laughingly told us that the Portuguese made the mistake of bringing together in Lisbon young Africans

* See excerpts from Cabral's Brazzaville speech on pp. 55–56.

## Amílcar Cabral: 'Cuban Revolution offers lessons for liberation struggles'

*From speech to Tricontinental Conference in Havana (January 1966)*

If any of us came to Cuba with doubts in our mind about the deep-rooted character, strength, maturity, and vitality of the Cuban Revolution, such doubts were dispelled by what we have already been able to see. Unshakable confidence warms our hearts and encourages us in this difficult but glorious struggle against the common enemy.

No power in the world will be able to destroy the Cuban Revolution, which is creating in the countryside and the cities not only a new life but—what is more important—a New Man, fully conscious of his national, continental, and international rights and duties. In every field of activity, the Cuban people have made significant progress over the past seven years.... This progress is demonstrated in material and daily reality and in Cuba's men and women, in their calm confidence as they face a world that is seething....

The vanguard of the Cuban Revolution has mobilized, organized, and politically educated the people, has kept them permanently informed about national and international questions that affect their lives, and has led them to take an active part in addressing those problems....

This constitutes a lesson for us, especially for the national liberation movements, and specifically for those who want their national revolution to be a true revolution....

National liberation struggles in the world today—especially in Vietnam, the Congo, and Zimbabwe—as well as the conflicts and upheavals in some countries that have gained independence through the so-called peaceful road, show us not only that compromises with imperialism are counterproductive, but that the normal road to national liberation, imposed on peoples by imperialist repression, is through armed struggle.

We are already fighting, arms in hand, against the Portuguese colonial forces in Angola, Guinea-Bissau, and Mozambique, and we are preparing to do the same in Cape Verde and São Tomé and Príncipe. For this reason we devote the closest attention to political work among our peoples, improving and constantly strengthening our national organizations.... That's why we are in Cuba attending this conference.

*From speech to Cuban internationalist combatants in Congo-Brazzaville (August 1966)*

I want to thank you on behalf of the leaders of the nationalist organizations in the Portuguese colonies for the fraternal welcome you've given us. It's a further demonstration of the active solidarity of the people and the [Communist] Party in Cuba.... It is clear evidence of the deep ties, not only historic but ties of blood, that bind Cubans to Africa.... I recall a conversation in Cuba with Fidel, who told me that Cuba is also Africa....

Barely ninety miles from [US shores], the Cuban people freed themselves from foreign domination and built their own country. And today, while they still have to solve their own problems, they are helping other peoples liberate themselves and build a nation. It's a unique example.

The PAIGC collaborates closely with the Cuban people and is very proud of that.... I guarantee you that we will completely defeat Portuguese colonialism in our country....

Our struggle is worth nothing if it's not deeply tied to those of other peoples in the Portuguese colonies. We consider all victories in Angola and Mozambique to be victories for Guinea as well....

I send our best wishes to your families, which are so far away. They must be proud of the effort and sacrifice you're making here to fulfill what Fidel said: "The entire world is a battlefield against imperialism."

from all their colonies—Angola, Mozambique, Guinea-Bissau, Cape Verde. They got to know each other and began to organize and discuss among themselves how to carry out the struggle for independence when they went back.

**DREKE:** You could say the Portuguese helped that process. Perhaps they were victims of their own prejudices. They couldn't grasp that there might be young people in their colonies who couldn't be bought, who would come together. That's where Amílcar met Agostinho Neto, who became the main leader of the MPLA in Angola's independence struggle.

After he returned to Bissau, Amílcar and other Guineans and Cape Verdeans founded the PAIGC in 1956 to launch a fight for independence from Portugal. They took part in trade union struggles. One was an important strike by the port workers, which was savagely repressed by the colonial forces. After that, they decided their movement had to wage an armed struggle to win their freedom.

**WATERS:** How did your participation in the Guinea-Bissau struggle begin?

**DREKE:** Soon after our return from the Congo in November 1965 I was designated head of Military Unit 1546, which was under the Ministry of the Interior. It provided military training to Cuban volunteers for internationalist missions abroad and to members of revolutionary groups from other countries, mostly from Latin America. In the 1960s combatants from a number of countries received military training in Cuba. We didn't give them political instruction. Each group had its own political views and we didn't interfere with that.

I was in that unit when Fidel asked me to head the military mission in Guinea-Bissau. He suggested I take some of the best men from the Congo campaign with me. Among those who went with me were Erasmo Videaux, Reynaldo Batista, and Eduardo Torres Ferrer—"Coqui." At Amílcar Cabral's request, most of the *compañeros* who went to Guinea-Bissau were black. That was so they would blend in with the population.

**WATERS:** How did you find the situation in Guinea-Bissau compared with the experience you had had in the Congo?

**DREKE:** The differences were apparent from the moment we arrived. It was clear that in Guinea-Bissau victory was possible.

The liberation war had advanced since it was launched in 1963. The Portuguese colonial regime had increased its military force from five thousand to twenty thousand, and they were brutal toward the civilian population. But when

I arrived the guerrilla fighters already controlled a third of the country. They had established liberated zones, where they organized and mobilized the population.

The struggle was led by the PAIGC, a strong, disciplined organization. Amílcar Cabral was its central leader. He had a clear political course of action and wide authority.

Amílcar succeeded in unifying the liberation movement in Guinea. He also united the Guinean fighters with the Cape Verdeans. This was very different from other African countries, where we unfortunately witnessed divisions within the liberation movements, especially divisions based on different ethnic groups.

**KOPPEL:** Cabral made a comment in 1972, two years before independence: “Ten years ago we were Fulas, Manjacos, Mandingas, Balantas, Pepels, and others. Now we are a nation of Guineans.” Can you say more about that?

**DREKE:** Amílcar was able to forge unity between the different ethnic groups. In Guinea the largest groups are the Balantas and the Fulas. There are also the others you mentioned, as well as the Bijagós, who are an island people.

Guineans and Cape Verdeans each have their own history and culture, but they fought together in a single organization for independence. João Bernardo Vieira—“Nino”—one of the most outstanding commanders, was Pepel. Aristides Pereira, the movement’s second-in-command under Amílcar, was Cape Verdean. After independence was won, he was elected the first president of Cape Verde.

Amílcar pressed for the broadest possible participation in the PAIGC. That contributed to the success of the independence struggle. As he said, through that struggle the nation of Guinea-Bissau was born.

# 2. First years of Cuba's internationalist mission

**WATERS:** What was the state of the struggle in Guinea-Bissau when you arrived?

**DREKE:** We arrived in February 1967. It was a critical moment. The first group of Cuban internationalists had been there since May of the previous year and after that the PAIGC intensified its actions. In November 1966 PAIGC combatants, accompanied by several Cuban compañeros, attacked the Portuguese garrison at Madina do Boé. The attack was repelled and they suffered heavy casualties. Domingos Ramos, the commander of the Eastern Front, was killed in combat. That loss created big difficulties. He was the first commander to fall in combat.

In response Fidel offered more assistance, which Amílcar accepted. With the reinforcement that I was part of, we soon had sixty compañeros. There were artillery instructors, doctors, drivers, and mechanics.

We established three training centers for the combatants. Our instructors didn't just teach. They fought side by side with the Guineans.

### 'We've got a little mission for you'

Fidel Castro sent for Víctor Dreke, veteran of the war against Batista and Guevara's right-hand man in Zaire [Congo] in 1965....

"Fidel told me: 'You have to take charge of the military mission in Guinea.'" He also urged Dreke to take some of the men who had been with him in Zaire, "the best."

A few days later, Dreke called on one of them, Erasmo Videaux, who was in charge of the UM [Military Unit] 1546 training camp in Baracoa.

"'How are you doing,' Dreke asked me," Videaux recalls. "'Fine,' I answered."

Dreke: "And your mother?"

Videaux: "Fine too."

Dreke: "We've got a little mission for you. You've got to get ready."

The next day Videaux flew to Santiago to say goodbye to his mother. "I told her I was going to take another course in the Soviet Union." (He had said the same when he had gone to Zaire.) "Our families were used to sudden departures."

—*From* Conflicting Missions: Havana, Washington, and Africa, 1959–1976, *by Piero Gleijeses*

Amílcar insisted from the beginning that he didn't want soldiers from other countries. He said Guineans had to fight the war themselves. They had to learn to defend their own country. If something didn't cost you much, you wouldn't defend it as tenaciously. But if you succeeded because of your own efforts, that was something you would defend.

Actually, that's what we did in our revolution in Cuba. We didn't ask anyone to free us. We did it ourselves—the Cuban people, led by Fidel and the Rebel Army.

Amílcar said, "No, I want only artillery instructors and doctors." Instructors because they had weapons but needed to learn to use the artillery. Doctors because they had none.

You have to remember that Portuguese colonialism had left Guinea-Bissau with nothing. Almost no schools, near total illiteracy. They had some nurses, but no Guinean doctors. Our doctors treated wounded combatants and provided health services to the civilian population in the liberated zones.

The guerrilla fighters had no trucks. We sent trucks, drivers, and mechanics, and they trained Guinean compañeros to drive and repair them.

One of our compañeros—he was known as Skinny Carlos—maintained and repaired the radio transmitter. He worked with Amélia Araújo, the presenter on Radio Libertação [Liberation], the PAIGC station that broadcast from Conakry. The radio broadcasts—in Portuguese, Creole, and other Guinean languages—were very important in reaching people, especially because of the high levels of illiteracy. They also directed broadcasts to the Portuguese soldiers, who were mostly conscripts, to explain why they too were victims of the Portuguese regime and had an interest in ending the war.

Most of the Cubans were artillery gunners. Some were specialists in laying land mines. They taught the guerrilla fighters to use mortars, bazookas, and other weapons they received from the Soviet Union.

**WATERS:** In his book *Conflicting Missions*, Piero Gleijeses says the battery chiefs needed to know advanced math to aim the artillery.

**DREKE:** Yes, the combatants were in the forest, and in that thick foliage they couldn't see the enemy directly. The Cape Verdeans in particular became very good artillery gunners. The battery chiefs were Cubans, because they needed to make mathematical calculations—trigonometry—to direct the mortars.

**WATERS:** How did the Cubans enter Guinea-Bissau?

**DREKE:** We entered through Guinea-Conakry, crossing the border into the Southern Front. To reach the Northern Front, it wasn't possible to enter from Senegal, because the government of Léopold Senghor—unlike Sékou Touré in Guinea-Conakry—wouldn't allow it.

The headquarters of the Cuban military mission was in Conakry. As head of the mission I frequently traveled to all three fronts inside Guinea-Bissau. To reach the north you had to cross the entire country from the south, going through the jungle.

**WATERS:** On foot?

**DREKE:** Mostly on foot. In many areas there was no other way to travel. To reach the north, near the border with Senegal, you had to cross the Farim River—now called the Cacheu—by boat. It was dangerous because Portuguese troops patrolled the river and sometimes ambushed rebel combatants while they were crossing.

On one occasion I was traveling with Pina, whom I'd named head of our combatants in the Northern Front. Pina—his real name is Alfonso Pérez Morales—had been part of the first group of Cubans to arrive in Guinea-Bissau. People said he was "almost Guinean." He had quickly learned to speak Creole like a native, and was well respected. Pina later became Cuba's first ambassador to an independent Guinea-Bissau.

In the late afternoon we reached a camp where Cuban combatants were stationed. It happened to be July 26, 1967, the anniversary of the assault on the Moncada barracks, a national holiday in Cuba. Pina proposed we go on to another camp, near the town of São Domingos, so we could celebrate together with the Guineans.

As we reached the second camp, the first one came under attack by the Portuguese. There's no doubt the PIDE, the Portuguese secret police, had knowledge about our presence from informers among the population.

That night we had a celebration—our fighters together with PAIGC fighters and villagers, many of whom were peasants. I gave a brief speech in Spanish about what we were celebrating, and Pina translated what I said to Creole. I still have a photo of that [see the sixth page of the first photo section in this book]. It was the first time we celebrated July 26 in a combat zone in Guinea-Bissau.

On our return trip, Pina and other compañeros accompanied us to the banks of the Farim River, which in some parts is very wide. Before we got there, a PAIGC unit combed the area to make sure it was safe.

We crossed to the other side by night, in a small boat, without an outboard motor to avoid making noise. We were able to cross without incident.

## "What does the Cuban Revolution teach? That revolution is possible." —SECOND DECLARATION OF HAVANA, 1962

GRANMA

**ABOVE:** Rebel Army combatants led by Fidel Castro enter Havana January 8, 1959, a week after Batista dictatorship was overthrown. The new revolutionary government mobilized working people to transform society and extend solidarity worldwide.

**BELOW:** At rally of one million, Castro presents Second Declaration of Havana, Feb. 4, 1962, after Washington imposed near-total ban on trade with Cuba. The manifesto was a call to action to anti-imperialist and revolutionary fighters across the Americas.

RADIO REBELDE

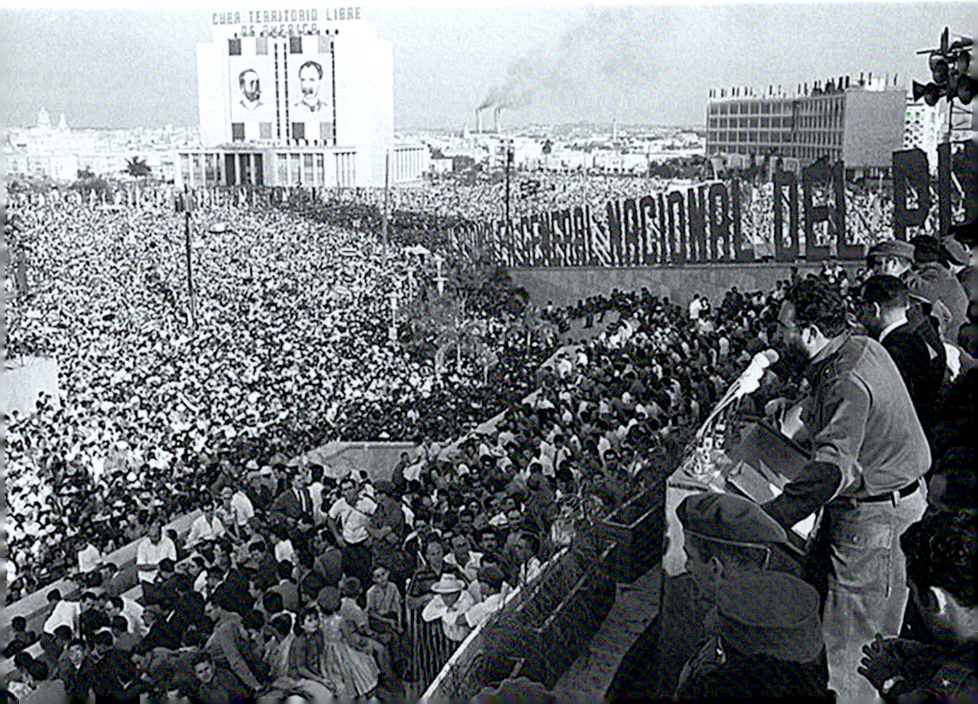

**"The Cuban people freed themselves from foreign domination. Today they are helping others liberate themselves. They are an outstanding example."**

—AMÍLCAR CABRAL, AUGUST 1966

COURTESY OF VÍCTOR DREKE

Eastern Front, Guinea-Bissau, 1967. Cuban combatants during independence war. Cabral told Cuban volunteers, "You are fulfilling what Fidel said: 'The entire world is a battlefield against imperialism.'"

COURTESY OF VÍCTOR DREKE

Northern Front, July 26, 1967. Víctor Dreke (center) addresses PAIGC combatants, villagers, and Cuban instructors. The event marked fourteenth anniversary of 1953 assault on Moncada garrison, which launched Cuba's victorious revolutionary war.

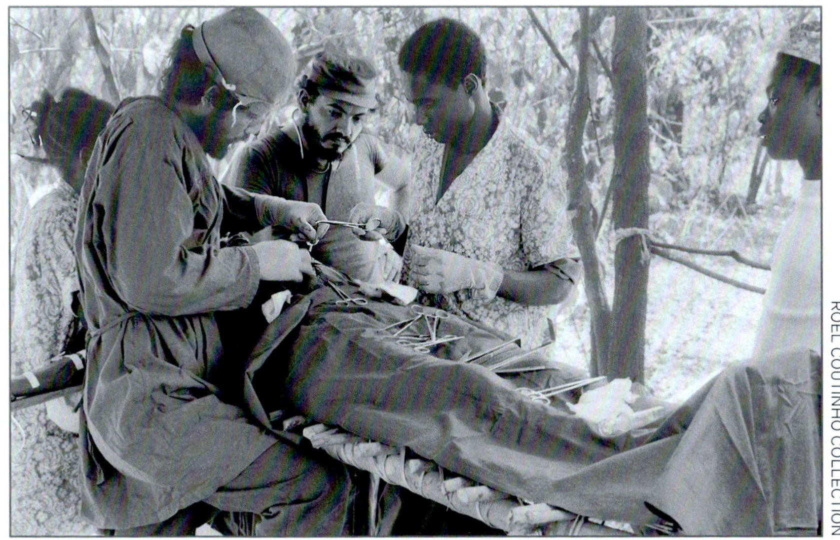
ROEL COUTINHO COLLECTION

Cuban doctor Domingo Díaz performs surgery and trains Guinean nurses in field hospital in Sará, Guinea-Bissau. The internationalist doctors "won the hearts of our fighters and our people," said PAIGC leader Luís Cabral.

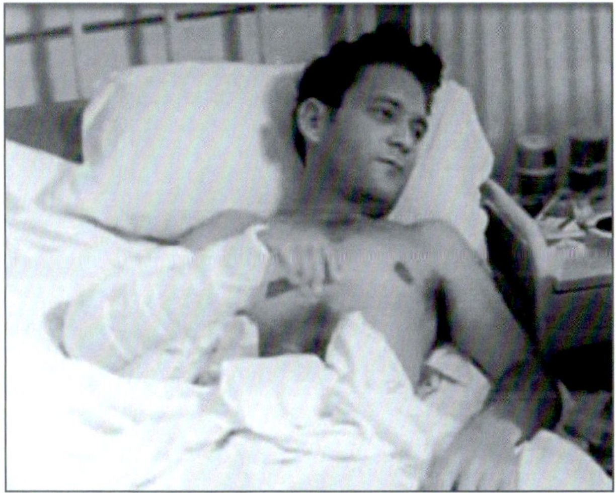

Cuban combatant Pedro Rodríguez Peralta in hospital after being captured by Portuguese army in Guinea-Bissau, 1969. Sentenced to ten years in a Lisbon prison, he was freed in 1974 with fall of Portugal's fascist regime. Rodríguez was later honored by Guinea-Bissau's government with the Amílcar Cabral Medal.

**“If there was a liberation movement in Africa with potential for victory, it was Amílcar Cabral’s African Party for the Independence of Guinea and Cape Verde. That was Fidel and Che’s view.”** —VÍCTOR DREKE

ARQUIVO LÚCIO LARA, ASSOCIAÇÃO TCHIWEKA DE DOCUMENTAÇÃO (LUANDA, ANGOLA)

Brazzaville, Republic of the Congo, January 1965. Che Guevara meets with Agostinho Neto (far right) and other MPLA leaders during three-month trip through Africa. Che also met with Cabral while in Conakry, Guinea.

FMSMB/CASA COMUM-AMÍLCAR CABRAL

Havana, January 1966. Amílcar Cabral and other PAIGC leaders at Tricontinental Conference attended by anti-imperialist fighters from around the world. From right, Cabral, Domingos Ramos, Pedro Pires, Joaquim Pedro Silva (“Baro”), and Vasco Cabral.

COURTESY OF VÍCTOR DREKE

After Tricontinental Conference, Fidel Castro invited Amílcar Cabral to visit Cuba's Escambray Mountains with him for three days. Fidel showed him how revolution had transformed living conditions in rural areas. He pledged to send artillery instructors, doctors, and mechanics to aid Guinean and Cape Verdean independence fighters.

Brazzaville, August 1966. Cabral speaks at camp where Cuban volunteers trained MPLA combatants for independence war in Angola. He thanked Cubans for their internationalist solidarity.

**“The Cuban Revolution has been internationalist from the start. Our first missions abroad were in Africa.”** —VÍCTOR DREKE

CIENCIAS SOCIALES

Ernesto Che Guevara with Cuban doctors and nurses in Algeria, July 1964. The Cuban government sent medical volunteers to newly independent Algeria, as well as combatants to help it deter a 1963 US-instigated attack by the regime in Morocco.

COURTESY OF VÍCTOR DREKE

Víctor Dreke (left) with Rafael Zerquera (center) and Che Guevara in the Congo, 1965. Guevara led 130 Cuban internationalists who joined Congolese anti-imperialist fighters. Dreke was second-in-command of the Cuban column.

EDITORA POLÍTICA

Cuban construction workers helping Vietnamese expand Ho Chi Minh Trail, 1974. Liberation fighters used it to transport troops and supplies during war against US invading forces, which were finally expelled by April 1975.

FLORIAN PLAUCHEUR/GETTY IMAGES

Cuban medical internationalists arrive in Freetown, Sierra Leone, October 2014. Within months, some 250 Cuban volunteers helped eradicate deadly Ebola epidemic in Guinea-Conakry, Liberia, and Sierra Leone.

**"Fidel insisted it's the leaders in each country who decide how to carry out their struggle. We have always respected those decisions. That was true in Guinea-Bissau."** —VÍCTOR DREKE

FMSMB/CASA COMUM-AMÍLCAR CABRAL

PAIGC delegation at event held at Cuban embassy in Conakry, Guinea, 1967. From left, Amílcar Cabral, Ana Maria Cabral, Víctor Dreke, Carlina Pereira, and Oscar Oramas, Cuba's ambassador to Guinea. Cabral asked for Cuban combatants to aid independence war "because he knew he could trust us," Dreke said. "We were comrades in struggle."

FMSMB/CASA COMUM-AMÍLCAR CABRAL

PAIGC combatants and Cuban internationalists. The Cubans were "a boost to our morale," said Commander Duke Djassi. "Here were men who had crossed the ocean to come to our aid. They lived with us, they shared in our sacrifices."

DERVIS ESPINOSA

Young PAIGC members, studying in Cuba, join voluntary agricultural work brigade, 1967.

JORGE FUENTES

Cuban instructor trains PAIGC combatants to aim 120 mm. mortar. These weapons were used in attack on Portuguese garrison of Guiledje, site of decisive battle in final offensive that defeated colonialist army, 1973.

**“Amílcar was committed to the goal that once Guinea-Bissau won its freedom, they would keep supporting the fight for Cape Verde’s independence.”** —VÍCTOR DREKE

AMÍLCAR CABRAL FOUNDATION, CAPE VERDE

Part of a group of Cape Verdeans, thirty men and a woman, undergoing military training in Cuba. In 1967 they returned to Africa, joining the guerrilla army in Guinea-Bissau.

Praia, Cape Verde, February 1975. Mass outpouring welcomes PAIGC leader Aristides Pereira home after victory in independence war. Pereira became country’s first president.

YUTAKA NAGATA/UN PHOTO

# 3. What we learned in Guinea-Bissau

**WATERS:** What were some of the things you learned from the struggle in Guinea-Bissau?

**DREKE:** We arrived with the experience we had gained in the Congo. We already had a little more knowledge about Africa, about the realities of colonial and imperialist rule. But every country has its own history and material conditions. I mentioned earlier some of the differences between the struggles in the Congo and in Guinea-Bissau. The movement led by Amílcar Cabral was a single organization, a united leadership with serious cadres. It fought to overcome the problems of tribalism we had seen in the Congo movement.

There were also differences between Guinea-Bissau and our experiences in the Cuban Revolution. We were impressed with the organization Amílcar had built. But we arrived with some ideas about the struggle that were different from his.

Fidel always insisted that it's the leaders in each country who decide how to carry out their struggle, and we must always respect those decisions. That's what we did. I would make suggestions to Amílcar; he would listen, without saying yes or no. Sometimes he followed my advice, sometimes he didn't. But he decided.

I'll give you some examples. One day the liberation movement decided to recruit a group of young people. They went into a village and took six young men and brought them to the camp. I didn't understand this. "How can you compel people to join?" I asked Amílcar. "You can't force people to fight. You have to convince them first." I told him that's what our experience had been in the Rebel Army.

Amílcar listened to me respectfully. Keep in mind he had lots of experience and I was a young person—not yet thirty—and new to that country. "What you're saying is true," he told me. "But that can't always be done here. Sometimes the *Tugas* [Portuguese soldiers] will come, forcibly take them away, and conscript them into the Portuguese army to fight against us. We have to incorporate them into our ranks before the Tugas do." The PAIGC, respecting the customs, would first talk to the village elder—the *homem grande*, or "big man"—and explain the situation. And then the village leader would usually give his consent for the youth to be recruited.

At the same time, Amílcar taught their cadres that they were above all a political, not a military, movement. The leaders always explained why they were fighting, what their political goals were. The combatants became conscious, dedicated fighters. Amílcar instilled moral values in them—that the PAIGC did not use methods of terror; that they did not commit abuses against civilians or enemy soldiers. This was different from what we saw in some other countries.

Amílcar was careful in how he deployed his cadres. He protected the military leaders. The movement faced very different circumstances from ours.

He would tell me, "In Cuba you have many commanders, many captains. But if they kill one of my commanders, it's very hard to replace him. Hardly any of our officers know how to read and write. And when I find an officer who can—and who is brave and the men respect—I have to protect his life."

As I mentioned before, Domingos Ramos, commander of the Eastern Front, was killed during the attack on the barracks at Madina do Boé. He was a man of great combative spirit, a member of the PAIGC's Political Bureau. He was also one of the few combatants who could read and write. Amílcar had to replace him with Nino Vieira, who was the commander of the Southern Front, and very capable. Taking Nino out of that front was a difficult decision.

**WATERS:** Was Cabral often in Guinea-Bissau?

**DREKE:** He came in and out of the country. Whenever there were important meetings or events, Amílcar organized and participated in them. He took part in some combat actions. He supervised every detail of the war and took responsibility for it, working closely with the commanders on the ground.

But Amílcar focused a lot on winning international support. These activities kept him from the front and from commanding military operations in person. That concerned us, because our training and experience taught us that the leader had to be at the front. That's the example that Fidel, Raúl [Castro], and Che gave us.

It was true, however, as the compañeros in the PAIGC would point out, that the struggle in Guinea-Bissau was not well known in the world. It was not like Vietnam. They had to break what Amílcar called "the wall of silence."

Cabral was the leader with the greatest authority and capacity to go to other countries and explain what they

**'We don't want a bloodthirsty people'**

At the beginning of our struggle there were comrades who suggested that within the scheme of our overall struggle, we should commit certain atrocities. But we rejected this. In our struggle there are none of those things that have occurred in other African countries. No matter what justification an African might give, is it a reason to kill women and children just because they are white?*

We have rejected this once and for all. Why? Because what we want is to carry out political resistance that serves our people. We don't want a bloodthirsty people, shedding blood for the sake of it. If blood is to be shed, it is for a political reason, to serve the future of our country.

*—Amílcar Cabral, speech to PAIGC cadres November 1969*

were fighting for, to denounce the atrocities the Portuguese were committing. He spoke to audiences and met with leaders in Africa, Europe, Asia, the United States. He spoke at the United Nations. That made it possible to win political support and material aid like weapons and medical supplies.

* In March 1961 Holden Roberto's National Front for the Liberation of Angola (FNLA), an organization—then known as the Union of African Peoples—that opposed Portuguese colonial rule, attacked farms in northern Angola. The group, based on the Bakongo tribe, slaughtered one thousand Portuguese settlers and six thousand indentured migrant workers belonging to the Ovimbundu tribe. The Portuguese army and armed settlers responded by destroying dozens of villages

In order to minimize losses, the PAIGC waged a war of attrition against the Portuguese. We preferred a more aggressive strategy, but we accepted their decisions. They wanted to avoid what had happened in that assault on Madina do Boé. "The Portuguese are not going to be able to sustain this war," he said. "Over time we're going to defeat them."

Amílcar would tell his commanders how many bullets to shoot. At first I wondered, why does he have to tell a military chief: "On this day, at this time, attack such-and-such a position. Fire twenty-five bazooka rounds and twenty mortar rounds." Actually, twenty would have been a lot. Often it was more like two or three.

When I asked Amílcar, he replied, "No, Moja. Here it's not like in Cuba. If I let our combatants fire, they'll shoot off all the ammunition. They have to learn."

"OK," I told him. "But when we were fighting Batista's army, we would capture weapons and ammunition from the soldiers."

"Yes," Amílcar replied, "we did that in the beginning. But now the Portuguese soldiers here no longer leave their garrisons. So how do we take their weapons?"

That was exactly what happened. The PAIGC controlled most of the countryside. So the Portuguese would launch air attacks, but the soldiers stayed inside the garrisons.

Amílcar always had an answer to our questions. As time went on, you saw that what he'd told you was accurate. He knew his country and he knew his people.

---

and killing twenty thousand residents. Cabral not only denounced the Portuguese bloodbath but condemned the massacre by the FNLA as "gratuitous violence."

After Angola won its independence in 1975, the FNLA, backed by Washington, allied itself with the South African apartheid regime's unsuccessful war to overthrow the MPLA-led Angolan government.

# 4. Relations of mutual respect

**WATERS:** In *Conflicting Missions*, author Piero Gleijeses quotes a Guinean commander, Duke Djassi, who said the Cubans were "a boost to our morale. They had crossed the ocean to come to our aid. They lived with us, they shared in our sacrifices." What can you add to this?

**DREKE:** Yes, our compañeros lived in the same camps with the Guinean combatants. We shared the food. We fought side by side. That brought us closer to the struggle. It enabled us to appreciate and better understand the Guinean people. We learned from each other.

Amílcar wouldn't let anyone impose their views on him about how to carry out the struggle. But he asked Fidel to send instructors and doctors—because he knew he could trust us. We were comrades in struggle.

**WATERS:** Was Cuba the only country that sent combatants?

**DREKE:** Yes. The PAIGC sought support from many countries. The Soviet Union, China, Czechoslovakia, and other countries gave them weapons, medical supplies, food, and scholarships. They also received material aid from Guinea-

Conakry, Algeria, Egypt, Yugoslavia, and Sweden. That aid was vital. But only our compañeros fought alongside the Guineans. That was Amílcar's decision.

The Cuban instructors trained the Guineans to use the Soviet weapons. On each of the three fronts a Cuban officer worked side by side with the PAIGC commander and served as an adviser.

Ulises Estrada, the Interior Ministry official in charge of our support to the PAIGC and other national liberation struggles in Africa, went to Guinea-Bissau. He was right next to Domingos Ramos during the battle of Madina do Boé when Domingos was killed by Portuguese fire. Ulises, who was almost killed himself, took Domingos's body in a truck across the border to Boké, in Guinea-Conakry, to make sure it didn't end up in Portuguese hands. It was a very risky action.

Conchita Dumois also went to Guinea-Bissau as an intelligence officer for the Interior Ministry. She was the first woman to be part of a Cuban military mission in Africa. At different points she was stationed in Madina do Boé and other guerrilla camps in the Eastern Front. I had a lot of respect for her.

**WATERS:** How many Cubans took part in the independence war?

**DREKE:** Between 1966 and 1974, when Guinea-Bissau won its independence, more than four hundred Cubans served there. Nine were killed in combat. One doctor, Miguel Ángel Zerquera, died of malaria.

In addition, one of our combatants, Captain Pedro Rodríguez Peralta, was captured and spent five years in Portuguese prisons.

**WATERS:** What happened to him?

**DREKE:** That was in 1969. I had already completed my mission and returned to Cuba. Erasmo Videaux, the second-in-command, had been appointed as my replacement.

Pedrito was on a reconnaissance patrol with a Guinean compañero. He hadn't taken a security detachment, which was a violation of Amílcar's orders that we should always be accompanied by security when leaving the camp on any mission. The Portuguese had received reports about Cubans in Guinea-Bissau and had been searching for us for some time.

The patrol was ambushed by Portuguese forces. The Guinean compañero was killed. Under fire, Pedrito held out until he was wounded and taken prisoner. They took him to Lisbon.

At the trial Pedrito stood firm as a revolutionary. He insisted he had joined the guerrilla struggle on his own. The prosecutor was unable to prove he had been sent by the Cuban government. They sentenced him to ten years in prison. He never broke.

After five years he was freed. It was after the Caetano dictatorship had fallen in the Carnation Revolution of 1974—in fact, just a week after Guinea-Bissau won its independence. On his return to Cuba he was welcomed by Fidel at the airport. Pedrito later worked in the Ministry of the Interior, with the rank of colonel, and was elected to the party's Central Committee. The government of Guinea-Bissau honored him with the Amílcar Cabral Medal.

**WATERS:** Luís Cabral, a leader of the independence struggle and the first president of Guinea-Bissau, said the Cuban doctors "won the hearts of our fighters and our people." Can you tell us more about that?

## Guineans and Cubans: Ties forged in battle

We were able to fight and triumph because other countries and people helped us, with weapons, with medicine, with supplies. But there is one nation that, in addition to material, political, and diplomatic support, even sent its children to fight by our side, to shed their blood in our land together with the best children of our country.

This great people, this heroic people, we all know it is the heroic people of Cuba. The Cuba of Fidel Castro. The Cuba of the Sierra Maestra, the Cuba of Moncada. Cuba sent its best children here, so they could help us wage this great struggle against Portuguese colonialism.

*—Luís Cabral, president of Guinea-Bissau*
*from 1977 speech awarding*
*Amílcar Cabral Order to Cuban combatant*
*Pedro Rodríguez Peralta*

The Cuban doctors in Guinea-Bissau "really performed a miracle. I am eternally grateful to them. Not only did they save lives, but they also put their own lives at risk. They were truly selfless."

*—Francisca Pereira*
*PAIGC leader and health official*

I came to this country as ambassador with firsthand knowledge of the difficult and glorious struggle you waged against Portuguese colonialism. My relationship with you did not begin with my appointment as ambassador. It was

> forged on the battlefield [as head of the Cuban volunteers in the Northern Front]. So I don't consider myself Cuba's first ambassador to Guinea-Bissau. The first ambassadors were those Cubans who volunteered to come here to make their modest contribution to your liberation struggle.
>
> *—Alfonso Pérez Morales ("Pina")*
> *from farewell speech as Cuban ambassador*
> *Bissau, June 1980*

**DREKE:** Before the Cuban internationalists arrived the PAIGC had no doctors inside Guinea-Bissau, and only a few nurses. Wounded combatants simply died. When the Cuban doctors arrived, they began to save many lives, and this boosted the morale of the combatants. They also improved conditions for the villagers in the liberated areas.

The doctors worked in small clinics or medical posts. Some worked in the PAIGC's hospital in Boké, Guinea-Conakry, along with a few doctors from other countries. In Guinea-Bissau the doctors were almost all Cubans.

In the Eastern and Southern Fronts, combatants who needed surgery were taken to Boké. Those in the north were taken to a small hospital the PAIGC had in the town of Ziguinchor, in southern Senegal, where a non-Cuban doctor worked. If surgery was required, a Cuban doctor would cross the border to Ziguinchor during the night, perform the operation, and go back to Guinea-Bissau before dawn. It was complicated, because the Senegalese government didn't allow Cubans into its territory. But our compañeros did that.

The Cuban doctors also taught classes and trained young Guinean women as auxiliary nurses. The first nurses were trained at the Boké hospital. The work was supervised by

## Championing women's equality and participation in liberation struggle

*The following are from talks and writings by Amílcar Cabral addressed to members of the African Party for the Independence of Guinea and Cape Verde or to Guinean villagers.*

Defend women's rights and make them respected. But convince the women of our country that their liberation must be through their own achievement, through their work, self-respect, character, and steadfastness in face of anything that goes against their dignity. (*1965*)

We are going to place women in high-ranking posts, and we want them at every level, from the village councils up to the party leadership. What for? To administer our schools and clinics, to take an equal share in production, and to go into combat against the Portuguese when necessary. . . . The women and girls will go into villages as nurses or teachers, or they will work in production, or in the village militia. . . .

Don't let anyone think these young women are up for sale as brides. They will get married if they wish, but there will be no forced marriages. Anyone who does that is worse than the Portuguese. (*1966*)

Some male comrades do their utmost to prevent women taking charge, even when there are women who have more ability to lead than they do. [They] do not want to understand that freedom for our people means women's liberation as well, that sovereignty for our people means women too must play a part, and

> that the strength of our party is greater if women join, as well as lead together with men. (*1969*)
>
> Our revolution cannot succeed without the full participation of women. (*1972*)

Carmen Pereira, one of the outstanding women leaders of the PAIGC, who was in charge of their public health department and was also responsible for political education in the Southern Front.

**KOPPEL:** What were conditions like in the liberated zones?

**DREKE:** They were difficult, of course. The Portuguese airplanes and helicopters carried out bombing raids to try to terrorize the population.

But the liberation movement had the support of the people. The PAIGC promoted participation in activities to improve conditions of life. Amílcar already had an idea of the country they were going to build after their victory. They began to create some elements of that structure in the liberated territories. That was different from what we had seen in the Congo or in some other national liberation struggles in Africa.

In addition to the small field hospitals and medical stations, they organized the population to set up schools. For the first time children were going to school. People not only learned to read and write. They began to conquer superstition and the fear of nature that were part of traditional beliefs.

The PAIGC organized local committees elected by the villagers. They administered things like health, education, and agricultural production. They ensured the equitable distribution of rice, the main food crop. Women played a big role in the village committees—two of the five members elected to the committees had to be women.

Amílcar gave a lot of importance to encouraging the participation of women. During the war, women not only carried out their traditional responsibilities of raising the family and doing the bulk of agricultural work. They transported weapons and served as nurses, teachers, political organizers, and diplomats. Some carried out intelligence work, and many were combatants, especially in the local militias. They helped persuade parents to overcome traditional barriers and send their daughters—not just their sons—to school.

A good number of women played leading roles. I mentioned Carmen Pereira and Amélia Araújo. Francisca Pereira was a PAIGC leader; after Guinea-Bissau gained independence she held important government positions.

And there was Titina—Ernestina Silá—who was head of a combat unit as well as the officer responsible for political education and organization in the Northern Front. She was greatly respected. After Amílcar Cabral was assassinated, Titina and other compañeros went to attend his funeral in Conakry. As they were crossing the Farim River, they were ambushed by a Portuguese patrol boat and Titina was killed. That day, January 30, 1973, is commemorated today as National Guinean Women's Day.

Young people and even children participated in the war. They carried mortars through the jungle. They hunted to get food for the guerrillas. A twelve-year-old boy would serve as a lookout, and when the Portuguese came, he would run to warn the fighters: "Here come the Tugas!" The boy learned what it took to be a combatant, and eventually they would give him a rifle and train him as a member of the guerrilla force.

**"We were able to win because other countries helped us. But one country even sent its children to fight by our side—the heroic people of Cuba."**

—LUÍS CABRAL, 1977

MILITANT

Havana, July 2006. Crispina Gomes, Cape Verde's ambassador to Cuba, presents Víctor Dreke with "Order of Amílcar Cabral" for his contribution to the war to free Cape Verde and Guinea-Bissau from colonial rule.

The order was signed by Cape Verde president Pedro Pires, a central leader of the independence struggle. In 1965 Pires had been part of a group of Cape Verdean combatants who received military training in Cuba.

# 5. Cape Verdeans in the independence war

**WATERS:** Tell us about the independence struggle in Cape Verde.

**DREKE:** Cape Verde had different conditions from Guinea-Bissau. The majority of the population in Cape Verde is *mestiço*, of mixed African and European ancestry. The Portuguese colonialists gave Cape Verdeans a little more access to education and to jobs. They tried to convince them they were "Portuguese," to divide them from the Guineans.

But the conditions on the islands remained miserable. The Portuguese did nothing to develop the economy. Cape Verde is arid, there is little agriculture, and they suffered terrible droughts and sometimes terrible famines. Because of these conditions, families to a large extent live from remittances sent by emigrants. More Cape Verdeans live abroad than in the country. Many live in Europe.

**KOPPEL:** There's also a significant Cape Verdean population in the United States, mostly in the Northeast—in Massachusetts and Rhode Island. Some have ancestors who worked on US whaling ships in the early 1800s.

**DREKE:** Despite the differences, Cape Verde and Guinea-Bissau have strong historical and cultural ties. Amílcar himself was born in Guinea-Bissau, but his parents were Cape Verdean. He went to school in Cape Verde. Amílcar was convinced that Guineans and Cape Verdeans could and should fight together for their independence.

After Che met him in 1965 and pledged Cuba's support, Amílcar traveled to European countries that had Cape Verdean communities. He recruited a group of students who went to Cuba for military training. The head of this group of thirty compañeros was Pedro Pires, who became prime minister when Cape Verde won its independence. Others included Abílio Duarte, Honório Chantre, and Manuel "Manecas" Santos, all of whom became leaders of the PAIGC.

The initial idea was for this group to return to Cape Verde and open up a guerrilla front there that would reinforce the struggle that had already begun in Guinea-Bissau.

They underwent intense training in the Escambray Mountains: long marches, swimming while carrying heavy backpacks, and so on. This was done under the direction of compañeros from Military Unit 1546, which, as I mentioned earlier, also trained our Cuban combatants for the mission in Guinea-Bissau.

Although Amílcar had sent these compañeros for training, after giving further attention to the conditions on the islands, he concluded that a guerrilla war there would not succeed.

Our view had been that armed struggle was possible in Cape Verde, based on the information we had. And that was my view initially. I hadn't been there yet; I visited the country later. But Cuba has always respected the sovereignty and decisions of revolutionary fighters in other countries.

Amílcar explained that the geographic conditions in Cape Verde weren't suitable for a guerrilla movement. They are volcanic islands. There are few trees. There are terrible droughts—sometimes it doesn't rain for five years. So there's little water or agriculture, no animals you can hunt for food. It's a small island country, far from the mainland.

In addition, most of the population wasn't ready for a war. Among other things, the majority of Cape Verdeans lived abroad. They wanted the Portuguese out, but the conditions didn't touch them as directly because they weren't living there.

When I went to Cape Verde some years later, I saw that Amílcar had been absolutely correct.

Amílcar proposed that the compañeros who had trained in Cuba to fight in Cape Verde instead join the guerrilla war in Guinea-Bissau. That's what they did.

The Cape Verdean compañeros played an important role in the war. Weapons had arrived from the Soviet Union and other countries. Our artillery instructors were training the Guineans. But the possibility opened up that the Cape Verdeans could take charge of the artillery. They had more schooling and had received training in Cuba with mortars and 75mm antitank cannon. So the Cape Verdeans, together with the Cubans, took responsibility for the heavy artillery.

While the war was unfolding in Guinea-Bissau, in Cape Verde the PAIGC did organize an underground movement and led trade union protests.

Amílcar was committed to the goal that once Guinea-Bissau won its freedom, they would keep supporting the fight for Cape Verde's independence. He was convinced the Portuguese would be forced to give it up, too.

That stance by Amílcar was important. He could have said, "If Guinea-Bissau is free, let the Cape Verdeans take care of their own problems." But he didn't. Amílcar didn't live to see it, but his strategy was proven correct. Both countries won their independence. They each established their own government.

# 6. Guinea-Conakry: Rear base for the war

**WATERS:** You led the Cuban military mission not only in Guinea-Bissau but in Guinea-Conakry. What was the place of that country in the events you are describing?

**DREKE:** Guinea-Conakry won its independence from France in 1958, under the leadership of Ahmed Sékou Touré. Ghana had won independence from British rule in 1957, and Guinea-Conakry became the second independent country in sub-Saharan Africa.

Even when I was there, the French imperialists had not forgiven Sékou Touré for the famous "No." In 1958 the government of Charles de Gaulle held a referendum to try to undercut the independence struggles sweeping Africa. France's African colonies were each given the option of voting "Yes" and remaining part of France. Or they could vote "No" and become independent. In Guinea, Sékou Touré campaigned for a "No" vote and "No" won a 95 percent majority. It was the first French colony to win independence, and Sékou Touré was elected its first president.

De Gaulle was furious. As they left, the French troops took everything they could—even the street lamps. They left the Guineans with nothing. But Sékou Touré became a hero throughout Africa.

A few years later, when the armed struggle began in Guinea-Bissau, Sékou Touré gave it vital support. He allowed Guinea-Conakry to serve as the rearguard for the guerrillas. Food supplies, weapons, and ammunition from Cuba, the Soviet Union, and other countries entered through Guinea-Conakry. So did our combatants and doctors. The PAIGC headquarters was in Conakry.

After Amílcar met with Fidel in Havana in 1966, Oscar Oramas, a compañero from our Foreign Ministry, was named Cuban ambassador to Guinea-Conakry and liaison with the PAIGC. When I was heading up the Cuban military mission, which was based in Conakry, I kept in direct communication with Sékou Touré, as well as with Amílcar Cabral and other PAIGC leaders.

**KOPPEL:** Did Cuba also provide assistance to Guinea-Conakry?

**DREKE:** Yes. We sent volunteer doctors and other aid. Remember that when the French left, they also took all their doctors. The Donka hospital, the only one in the country at the time, had to shut down. Ever since then, we've had Cuban doctors working in Guinea. Hundreds of Guinean students have received scholarships to study medicine and other fields in Cuba.

Fidel's first visit to Africa was to Conakry in 1972. He met with Sékou Touré and pledged to increase our aid. Cuba offered more scholarships. We sent construction workers to build airports and pilots to train Guineans to fly a few MiGs they had received from the Soviet Union.

**WATERS:** Cuba also trained militias in Guinea-Conakry. How did that come about?

**DREKE:** Sékou Touré decided to organize militias to help defend the Guinean government against any assault by the Portuguese, who wanted to deny the PAIGC its rearguard base in Guinea-Conakry. And to defend against any destabilization attempt by the French government. He asked us to train the new militia units.

So, in addition to the volunteers who went to Guinea-Bissau, we brought instructors to train the militias in Conakry. Those Cuban compañeros would also be deployed periodically to the war fronts in Guinea-Bissau, rotating in and out, to give them experience.

We agreed it was important to prepare the Guinean people, not just the army, to defeat any imperialist attack. Sékou Touré had a lot of popular support. In later years he changed, and problems developed—that's another story.

But it wasn't enough to have popular support. The people had to be armed and trained.

As it turned out, training of the militias kept getting delayed. Some of Guinea's military leaders didn't want the militias. They didn't say so, of course, but it was clear they didn't. There were tensions within the Guinean government and armed forces, and Sékou Touré was concerned some of the high military officers might try to overthrow him.

Colonel Kaman Diaby was the deputy army chief of staff; he had been trained in the French army when Guinea was still a colony. My relations with him were good. We would talk about preparations for the militia training, and whenever I asked, the answer was always: "Yes, everything's

**"Cuban volunteers trained militias in Guinea-Conakry to defend its government from any Portuguese attack. That country was the PAIGC's rear guard."** —VÍCTOR DREKE

COURTESY OF VÍCTOR DREKE

Dreke presents bazooka to President Ahmed Sékou Touré of Guinea during governing party's 1967 congress. It was a symbol of Cuba's commitment to train militias to protect the government against Lisbon-backed coup threats.

COURTESY OF VÍCTOR DREKE

Cuban instructors train militia members in Conakry, 1967. Dreke, in charge of the trainers, is on the right.

ready. The bazookas are in the garrison." Those were the forty bazookas we had given them for the militias.

"We'll start tomorrow," Diaby would say. But then it was the day after, and the day after, and still the training didn't begin.

Sékou Touré was trying to find a way for the militias to be trained by us in collaboration with the armed forces, so no one could argue that the militias were counterposed to the army. That was important. But there was resistance within the army command.

After many delays, we talked with Sékou Touré. "Mr. President," I said, "you want the militia training to start. We need your support to do so." The president seemed tormented about how to respond, but he finally said, "OK, start whenever you want to."

"Perfect," I said. "We'll start in the next few days, Mr. President. When you hear shots being fired, it will mean the training has begun."

And that's what we did. We started by having the trainees fire into the ocean. Of course, it set off a commotion when people heard the shots. But the president had told us to go ahead. If we hadn't taken that initiative, it never would have happened. We ended up training more than a thousand militia members.

**KOPPEL:** There is a photo of you, dressed in olive green, giving Sékou Touré one of the forty bazookas you mentioned.

**DREKE:** That was at a congress in 1967 of the ruling party, the Democratic Party of Guinea. I was an invited guest, representing the Cuban Communist Party's Central Committee, of which I was a member. When I spoke at the congress, I presented the bazooka to Sékou Touré on behalf of

Fidel and our leadership. It was a symbol of Cuba's commitment to train the militias.

**WATERS:** There was, in fact, an attempt by the Portuguese military to overthrow Sékou Touré's government in November 1970. What did the militias do at that time?

**DREKE:** By then I had already returned to Cuba, but I followed the events closely. The Portuguese government organized a commando raid in Conakry. They wanted to overthrow Sékou Touré and to capture or kill Amílcar Cabral. It was a desperate move, since they were losing the war.

Some four hundred men landed on the beaches of Conakry—soldiers of the Portuguese army, including African troops, together with Guinean mercenaries. They tried to seize some government facilities and the PAIGC headquarters.

But the attack was defeated. Loyal Guinean troops were mobilized, together with the militias we had trained and PAIGC combatants who were in Conakry. In addition, Cuban combatants who were near the border were deployed to Conakry as reinforcements. This had been planned beforehand, since a Portuguese attack was expected.

Some of the invaders fled and others were captured. Afterward, the government executed several high government officials accused of taking part in the plot. Some were hanged, before a massive audience, from a bridge in Conakry, something the Cuban Revolution has never done and would never do.

In historical accounts that have been published, the Cuban role in training militias in Guinea-Conakry is seldom mentioned. But it was important.

**RÓGER CALERO:** In Cuba there is no contradiction between the armed forces and the militias, because you made a socialist revolution and you have a revolutionary army.

**DREKE:** That's right. In Cuba the militias played a vital role in the defense of the revolution from the beginning. They are the armed people. They are not in conflict with the Revolutionary Armed Forces. In fact, they were created by the Rebel Army, at the initiative of Fidel.

# 7. Portuguese colonialism is defeated

**WATERS:** You returned from Guinea-Bissau in late 1968. Piero Gleijeses quotes US government cables noting that by the end of that year, the position of the forces led by Cabral in Guinea-Bissau had improved significantly.

**DREKE:** I think that's correct. The artillery gunners had been training with the Cuban instructors, and they were good, disciplined combatants. Apart from the cities, the majority of the country by then was controlled by the guerrilla movement.

The Portuguese government was having more and more problems with its war. Eventually they increased their military presence there to forty thousand troops, several thousand of them Africans from Portugal's different colonies.

It was not a popular war. More and more Portuguese soldiers were deserting. The PAIGC would turn the captured soldiers over to the Red Cross. They would tell these young men, "Our war is not with the Portuguese people, it's with the government in your country. We have the same enemy." Portuguese civilians they captured were not mistreated; they were released.

By the way, Amílcar insisted that after independence was won, it was important to promote the use of the Portuguese language, to learn to speak it well. Not only as a common language within Guinea-Bissau and Cape Verde, but as a way to communicate with people in Portugal and other Portuguese-speaking countries. To reach people around the world.

To deal with its growing crisis, the regime in Lisbon named a new military commander for "Portuguese" Guinea, General António de Spínola. He launched a propaganda campaign to undercut popular support for the liberation movement. For the first time, the Portuguese started building some schools and clinics in the territories they controlled to try to convince people they were improving living conditions. At the same time, they stepped up the bombing of villages. It was a campaign of "smiles and blood," as Amílcar called it.

**CALERO:** Although they denied it, the US government supported the Portuguese colonial wars in Africa. The Kennedy, Johnson, and Nixon administrations all sold fighter jets and other military equipment to the Portuguese regime on condition—officially—that they not be used in Africa. But of course they were. They gave Lisbon millions as "payment" for use of Portugal's air force base in the Azores islands. In fact, as Cabral told the United Nations in 1972, because of its weakness as an imperialist power, "Portugal would not be able to wage three simultaneous wars in Africa without the aid of its allies."

**DREKE:** The US sold weapons to Portugal as a NATO ally. But the Portuguese military used those weapons in Guinea-Bissau, Angola, and Mozambique, and the US government turned a blind eye.

**KOPPEL:** In 1972 Fidel sent Commander Raúl Díaz Argüelles to Guinea-Bissau to work closely with the PAIGC leadership in the liberation war.

Díaz Argüelles is a hero for the Cuban people—and for many Africans. He is especially known for his outstanding role at the beginning of Cuba's internationalist mission in Angola, where he fell in combat in 1975.

Not much is known about his leadership in the earlier war in Guinea-Bissau, however. Can you tell us about that?

**DREKE:** The fact that Fidel sent Commander Díaz Argüelles reflected the importance our revolutionary leadership gave to the struggle in Guinea-Bissau, which at that point was at a critical stage.

In April 1972 the 10th Directorate of the Revolutionary Armed Forces was created to direct all of our international military missions, and Argüelles was named to head the Directorate. Until then, those missions had been organized through the Ministry of the Interior.*

Argüelles visited the liberated zones in Guinea-Bissau together with commanders of the PAIGC to assess the situation. The liberation movement was in a strong position, and it was time to deal decisive blows to the Portuguese army. Our experience during the revolutionary war in Cuba

* Cuba's military missions abroad, including in Guinea-Bissau and Guinea-Conakry, were initially organized through a department of the Ministry of Interior called Dirección 5, headed by Ulises Estrada. That department was under the ministry's General Intelligence Directorate (DGI), headed by Commander Manuel Piñeiro. In April 1972 the Revolutionary Armed Forces (FAR) took charge of all internationalist military missions, for which it created the 10th Directorate, headed by Raúl Díaz Argüelles. Missions involving not just instructors but military troops—such as Angola starting in 1975, Ethiopia in 1977, and Nicaragua in 1979—were led directly by the FAR's general staff.

had been that whenever we had the capacity to take the army's garrisons, we'd do so.

Argüelles reported his conclusions to our leadership. And then, with Fidel's backing, Argüelles proposed to Amílcar to launch an operation against Portuguese garrisons.

The PAIGC's strategy had been to wage a war of attrition against the Portuguese forces. The enemy still maintained air superiority and, as I mentioned before, Amílcar was trying to minimize the losses of his cadres. He was convinced it was a matter of months before the Portuguese colonialists would be forced to concede independence. They were facing growing problems with their war, as well as international pressure.

Amílcar considered the Cuban proposal to launch an offensive against Portuguese bases, however. And he eventually accepted it. But that campaign had not begun before he was assassinated.

**CALERO:** Cabral was assassinated in Conakry in January 1973 in an operation organized by the Portuguese secret police and carried out by former PAIGC members who had been recruited by the Portuguese. How did that affect the struggle?

**DREKE:** The Portuguese were losing the war. They killed Cabral hoping to deal the struggle a mortal blow. But they didn't succeed. The movement Amílcar had forged was an experienced political and military force with strong roots in the population. Aristides Pereira, the second-in-command, was chosen to replace Amílcar as the PAIGC's general secretary.

**CALERO:** In December 1972, shortly before his death, Cabral had visited Moscow, where he finally won agreement from the Soviet government to provide portable

**"During the war, women not only carried out their traditional responsibilities. Many served as nurses, teachers, political organizers, and combatants."** —VÍCTOR DREKE

Titina Silá, PAIGC leader and head of a combat unit on the Northern Front. Killed by Portuguese forces in 1973, she is a national hero in Guinea-Bissau.

FMSMB/CASA COMUM-AMÍLCAR CABRAL

PAIGC nurses worked in liberated zones as well as in rebel hospitals across the border in Boké, Guinea, and Ziguinchor, Senegal.

FMSMB/CASA COMUM-AMILCAR CABRAL

Carmen Pereira, PAIGC leader, addresses combatants in liberated area.

**“The victory in Guinea-Bissau precipitated the end of the fascist dictatorship in Lisbon and the collapse of Portugal’s colonial empire.”**

—VÍCTOR DREKE

New York, January 22, 1973. Demonstration against Amílcar Cabral’s assassination and US military aid to Lisbon’s colonial wars. Protests were also held in other US cities.

SOUTHERN AFRICA MAGAZINE

London, July 1973. Thousands protest visit of Portuguese dictator Marcelo Caetano and Lisbon’s colonial rule in Africa.

©NLA REPORT DIGITAL

Guinea-Bissau, liberated territory, September 24, 1973. Delegates to National Popular Assembly vote to proclaim independence. Portugal recognized the new republic a year later.

FMSMB/CASA COMUM-INEP

ALAMY

Lisbon, April 1974. Thousands celebrate overthrow of Portugal's fascist regime. The "Carnation Revolution" set off mass revolutionary upsurge and, by the end of 1975, helped ensure independence of all Portuguese colonies in Africa.

FAUSTO GIACCONE

Rural workers on their way to a land occupation, Ribatejo, Portugal, 1975. Similar struggles for land took place across the country.

Lisbon, November 12, 1975. Thousands of construction workers mobilize outside parliament. Deputies were not allowed to leave until they agreed to a union contract with a much-needed 40 percent wage raise.

FMSMB/CASA COMUM/©CARLOS GIL/SPA, LISBON 2025

**"In turning over Portuguese prisoners of war to the Red Cross, we call attention to the crimes of the Portuguese colonialists."** —AMÍLCAR CABRAL, MARCH 1968

**RIGHT:** Captured Portuguese soldiers being released to Red Cross in Senegal, March 1968. The PAIGC told them, "Our enemy is colonialism, not the Portuguese people."

FMSMB/CASA COMUM-AMÍLCAR CABRAL

FMSMB/CASA COMUM-INEP

**LEFT:** One of the many napalm bombs used by Lisbon's forces to maim and terrorize the civilian population.

**BELOW:** Cabral with young guerrillas, 1972. "He instilled moral values in them—that they were above all a political, not a military, movement," Dreke said. "That they did not commit abuses against civilians or Portuguese soldiers."

FMSMB/CASA COMUM-AMÍLCAR CABRAL

Cuban commander Raúl Díaz Argüelles (dark glasses) with Cuban and Guinean fighters. Argüelles worked closely with guerrilla commanders in leading final offensive in 1973-74.

COURTESY OF VÍCTOR DREKE

**"The Portuguese army was completely demoralized by its defeats in Guinea-Bissau. Cuba played a decisive role in the PAIGC's final battle victories."** —VÍCTOR DREKE

FMSMB/CASA COMUM-AMÍLCAR CABRAL

Portuguese warplane shot down in eastern Guinea-Bissau. In 1973, Cuban-trained artillery gunners destroyed Lisbon's air superiority.

PAIGC combatants seize Guiledje garrison after Portuguese troops were routed, May 1973. Battle was turning point in the liberation war.

FMSMB/CASA COMUM-AMÍLCAR CABRAL

**"Amílcar already had a view of the society they wanted to build after the victory. They established schools, hospitals, and village committees in the liberated territories."** —VÍCTOR DREKE

ROEL COUTINHO COLLECTION

FMSMB/CASA COMUM-INEP

**TOP:** School in liberated area, 1974. Thousands of Guinean children and adults "not only learned to read and write. They began to conquer superstition and fear of nature that were part of traditional beliefs," said Dreke.

**BOTTOM:** Leaders of seventeen village committees meet in a liberated zone. Elected by villagers, the committees administered health, education, agricultural production, justice, and other local affairs. Women took important responsibilities in the committees.

FMSMB/CASA COMUM-AMÍLCAR CABRAL

Amélia Araújo reporting on PAIGC's Liberation Radio. The station provided information and helped educate combatants and the population. It also broadcast to Portuguese soldiers, explaining why they too were victims of the Lisbon regime and had an interest in ending the war.

FMSMB/CASA COMUM-INEP

Contingent of health workers marches in celebration held in liberated territory when PAIGC proclaimed an independent republic, September 1973. During the war, clinics and hospitals provided medical care to the population for the first time.

**"After a 16-year war, the Angolan people, backed by Cuban internationalists, defeated the South African invaders. This victory accelerated the fall of the white-supremacist regime."** —VÍCTOR DREKE

Cuito Cuanavale, Angola, 1988. Cuban and Angolan combatants on captured South African tank celebrate battle victory. Between 1975 and 1991, some 425,000 Cuban volunteers helped ensure Angola's sovereignty.

Nelson Mandela and Fidel Castro in Matanzas, Cuba, July 1991. The Cuban internationalists made an "unparalleled contribution to African independence, freedom, and justice," Mandela said.

MARY-ALICE WATERS/MILITANT

surface-to-air missiles that could shoot down planes. Gleijeses notes in *Conflicting Missions* that by March 1973, when Guinean combatants had been trained to use this equipment, the missiles changed the military situation to the advantage of the Guinean combatants. Can you say more about that?

**DREKE:** The arrival of these antiaircraft weapons tipped the relationship of forces in favor of the liberation movement. Until then, Portuguese planes had been able to fly close to the ground. They strafed villages and dropped napalm that destroyed crops and burned many civilians. Under those conditions, it was very difficult to attack the Portuguese garrisons.

Now, with the new antiaircraft missiles—the *Flechas* ["arrows" in Spanish], as we called them—the guerrillas for the first time began to shoot down the planes. They were able to protect both the combatants and the civilian population. It was a group of Cape Verdean artillery gunners we had trained, headed by Manecas Santos, a PAIGC leader, together with the Cuban instructors, who fired the Flechas.

The Portuguese were stunned. Their pilots were afraid, and no longer wanted to go out on missions. This had a big impact on the course of the war. After several planes were shot down, the Portuguese stopped sending their pilots into combat zones, or they would fly very high, out of range of the artillery.

Argüelles—again, with Fidel's strong support—renewed his proposal to the PAIGC leadership to launch an offensive against the Portuguese garrisons, and they agreed.

In May 1973 "Operation Amílcar Cabral" was launched. By then the guerrilla army had about eight thousand combatants. The campaign was planned and led jointly by Commander Nino and Argüelles. About forty Cuban compañeros took part in the different battles in the north and the south.

## Captured Portuguese soldiers treated with dignity

In our struggle for national independence, peace, and progress for our people in Guinea and the Cape Verde Islands, the freeing of Portuguese soldiers captured by our armed forces was necessary and to be expected.... We are not fighting against the Portuguese people, or against Portuguese individuals or families. Without ever confusing the Portuguese people with colonialism, we have had to take up arms to wipe our homeland free of the shameful rule of Portuguese colonialism....

Members of our armed forces captured by the colonial troops are generally subject to a summary execution. Others are tortured and forced to make declarations that the colonial authorities use in their propaganda.... The Portuguese colonialists engage in acts of terrorism against the peaceful inhabitants of our liberated areas daily, particularly against women, children, and the elderly. They bomb and machine-gun our people, reduce our villages to ashes, and destroy our crops. They use bombs of every type, particularly fragmentation bombs, napalm, and white phosphorus.

In turning over these Portuguese prisoners of war [to the Red Cross in Senegal], we once again call the attention of world opinion to the crimes perpetrated in our country by the Portuguese colonialists.... Portuguese public opinion, especially among the popular masses and in intellectual circles, is becoming more aware each day of the necessity of taking action by every available means against the colonial war.

*—Amílcar Cabral*
*Dakar, Senegal, March 1968*

◆

The freeing of three more Portuguese prisoners of war at Christmas is nothing new; it's our policy.... We conveyed to the three released prisoners our desire that they rejoin their families, and that they speak to them about us, so that, despite the crimes of the colonial government, the ties between our people and the people of Portugal can be maintained....

The Portuguese government has no consideration for its own people, to whom it tells gross lies, or for the young men who, at the cost of their own lives and other sacrifices, are fighting without glory in a criminal war in our country.

We believe a prisoner of war deserves respect, because he is giving his life, whether or not the cause he is fighting for is just. For this reason we call on the people and patriots of Portugal to force the government to respect the people it rules, and to respect the elementary international norms regarding prisoners of war.

*—Amílcar Cabral, radio broadcast*
*January 1969*

Now that the enemy planes were less of a threat, the combatants launched a direct assault on the Guiledje garrison, the most important one in the south. Hundreds of PAIGC fighters took part in that battle, together with a contingent of Cubans.

The Portuguese suffered heavy casualties. They withdrew from the base, and the combatants captured Guiledje. It was a resounding victory. In the following months the Portuguese abandoned other garrisons.

**KOPPEL:** Leaders of the PAIGC have pointed out that they were also making gains on the political front. They exposed Lisbon's brutality at international forums in the United States and Europe. A UN delegation visited liberated areas and condemned the Portuguese army's bombing of civilians. In mid-1972, Guineans in the liberated territories, after a process of months of discussions, voted in their first elections, choosing 120 deputies for a new National Popular Assembly. Then in September 1973, as they were achieving military victories, the National Assembly proclaimed an independent Republic of Guinea-Bissau, which won wide international recognition.

**DREKE:** The international support for Guinea-Bissau was important, since the Portuguese regime depended on the US, West Germany, and other NATO powers for military aid to sustain their wars in Africa.

The victory of the Vietnamese people, who drove out the US military forces and reunified their country, also had a big impact. It weakened imperialism on a world scale, including the Portuguese imperialists.

**WATERS:** As we know from our own experiences in the United States, it was a time when millions around the world were being drawn into political activity in support of the victorious battles of the Vietnamese people. Washington's use of massive military might to try to defeat the Vietnamese opened the eyes of a new generation of young people to the realities of imperialism.

**DREKE:** Yes, and there were growing protests against Portugal's colonial wars, not only in Portugal itself but in the United Kingdom and other countries.

The Portuguese army had become completely demoralized by its defeats in Guinea-Bissau. This accelerated the collapse of the colonial regime itself.

In response to this crisis, the military command deposed the Caetano government in a coup. That sparked the Carnation Revolution. You can see photos of the hundreds of thousands of people in the streets of Lisbon, celebrating the fall of the dictatorship. After fifty years of a fascist regime, they wanted freedom. Workers and peasants were demanding their rights.

The coup in Portugal took place in April 1974. A few months later, in September, the new government recognized the independence of the Republic of Guinea-Bissau.

And a little more than a year later, in July 1975, the independence of Cape Verde was proclaimed. Amílcar's promise was fulfilled. Even if Guinea-Bissau won its independence first, the PAIGC would not abandon the people of Cape Verde, and they would win their freedom too.

The same year, Mozambique and Angola won their independence, as did São Tomé and Príncipe.

# 8. International impact of the victory

**WATERS:** How do you see the international impact of the victorious independence struggle in Guinea-Bissau?

**DREKE:** That victory was a turning point in Africa. It was the detonator that brought down the Portuguese colonial empire. And it led to the end of the dictatorship in Portugal itself.

Guinea-Bissau showed how a small African country—with a population of half a million at the time, with very little economic development, and a liberation army with few weapons and resources—could defeat an imperial power and a much greater military force.

Amílcar Cabral himself came to symbolize for millions around the world the best qualities of an anti-imperialist leader. He identified with liberation struggles not only in Africa but around the world. He instilled confidence in the people of Guinea-Bissau and Cape Verde that they could fight and win. In clear words, he would explain what they were fighting for and the moral values that would enable them to win.

The Guinean population actively participated in that struggle. They were led by a strong political movement. It wasn't just a guerrilla army.

The victory in Guinea-Bissau was an inspiration to anti-imperialist struggles throughout Africa, especially in Angola and Mozambique. Those two colonies of Portugal won their independence the following year, in 1975, although it would take many more years for them to secure their sovereignty.

After a war lasting a decade and a half, in 1988 the Angolan people—backed by internationalist Cuban combatants—defeated the South African troops that had invaded their country.

That victory inspired the people of South Africa, who, as Nelson Mandela said, were fighting for "a democratic, nonracial South Africa." They put an end to the white-supremacist regime.

It was worth fighting—that's the lesson we can learn. And for the Cubans who went to Guinea-Bissau and other African countries, taking part in those internationalist missions was worth it.

**WATERS:** What has been the impact in Cuba of the fact that hundreds of thousands of Cubans have taken part in internationalist missions in Africa over the decades? Some 425,000 in Angola alone, between 1975 and 1991.

**DREKE:** Those who have served in Africa have brought back their experiences. Our combatants learned a lot from the people of Guinea-Bissau, with whom we shared everything. The same with the Cuban doctors who have worked in the most difficult places. They've cared for people and won their trust.

### Fidel Castro: 'African independence struggles helped spark Carnation Revolution in Portugal'

In Portugal, a fascist government had ruled for more than forty years. It carried out a ten-year war against those fighting for the independence of the Portuguese colonies in Africa. But that very struggle by the patriots of Guinea-Bissau, Angola, and Mozambique led Portuguese colonialism and fascism to a crisis. First to an international crisis in which the government became isolated and discredited, and finally to an internal crisis.

That is, in fighting for independence, the Africans helped the Portuguese people. It was an element that helped give birth to the Portuguese revolution. Without the struggle in Portugal's African colonies, it's possible the April 25 [1974] revolution in Portugal would never have occurred, or it would have taken much longer to develop.

And, in turn, the events in Portugal helped accelerate the independence of those African countries.

*—Fidel Castro*
*September 1975*

The Cuban people have developed affection and respect for our African brothers and sisters. We say that African blood runs in our veins. You can see this every day in our culture, in our lives. It doesn't matter whether your skin color is lighter or darker. There's an African presence in all of us.

In Africa, as in other parts of the world where Cuban internationalists have served, we've seen firsthand the extreme poverty in which a great part of humanity lives. We've learned more about imperialist exploitation. You're not just reading about the exploitation of man by man in books by Marx or Lenin. You've seen it, you've lived it.

Today Cuban internationalist volunteers continue to work in many African countries: doctors, nurses, teachers, technical specialists. And thousands of African youth have graduated from medical schools here in Cuba.

Cuban internationalists have also established medical schools in several African countries. The first one in sub-Saharan Africa was in Guinea-Bissau, which was founded in 1986 by the Cuban medical mission there, headed by Dr. Ana Morales Valera. It's named after Commander Raúl Díaz Argüelles.

More recently, Cuban medical volunteers played a decisive role in 2014–15 in ending the Ebola epidemic in Liberia, Sierra Leone, and Guinea-Conakry.

Our biggest internationalist mission was in Angola, where, as I mentioned, over sixteen years, our combatants joined with the Angolans to defeat multiple invasions by the South African army. They had a decisive weight in defending the sovereignty of Angola and winning the independence of Namibia. And those victories contributed to the end of the apartheid regime itself.

Fidel always explained that, unlike the imperialist powers, we didn't go to Africa to plunder the natural resources and exploit human beings. He popularized a remark that Amílcar Cabral had made earlier. As Fidel put it:

"Cuba did what the famous anti-colonialist leader Amílcar Cabral said it would do: 'The Cuban combatants are ready to sacrifice their lives to free our countries. And in exchange for that aid to our freedom and the progress of our peoples, the only thing they will take away with them are their combatants who fell in the fight for freedom.'"

That's what happened.

Our internationalist experiences strengthened the consciousness and confidence of the Cuban people. As Raúl said, thanks to Angola—and we could add Guinea-Bissau—the Cuban people "know much better what we are capable of achieving."

# ‘It was a matter of pride to be asked to go on an internationalist mission’

VOICES OF OTHER CUBAN COMBATANTS

# ‘It was a matter of pride to be asked to go on an internationalist mission’

## VOICES OF OTHER CUBAN COMBATANTS

*By Martín Koppel, Mary-Alice Waters, and Róger Calero*

“WHY DID WE GO TO AFRICA? Why did Cubans join combat missions in the Congo, or Guinea-Bissau, or Angola?” asked Alfonso Pérez Morales, a lieutenant colonel in Cuba’s Revolutionary Armed Forces (FAR), now retired.

“When I signed up, in 1965, the Cuban Revolution had triumphed just six years earlier,” he said in a February 2025 interview in Havana. “The Cuban people, led by Fidel, had brought about profound changes in our society. We felt a strong identification with people fighting imperialist domination in other parts of the world. Many of us responded to Fidel’s appeal to join internationalist missions in Africa, Latin America, and Asia.”

Better known by his nom de guerre Pina, Pérez Morales was introduced to us by Víctor Dreke as work on this book was being completed.

In the pages you’ve just been reading, Dreke describes how Pina was part of the initial group of Cuban internationalists who went to Guinea-Bissau as military instructors or doctors. The two worked closely together, Dreke as head of Cuba’s military mission based in Conakry, and Pina as leader of the Cuban volunteers serving in the Northern Front alongside guerrillas of the PAIGC.

After his first stint in 1966–68, Pérez Morales returned to Guinea-Bissau in 1972 for what became the final two years of the liberation war. When Guinea-Bissau won independence from Portugal in 1974, Pina was named Cuba's first ambassador to that country.

We also spoke with other Cuban internationalists who were part of Cuba's mission in Guinea-Bissau: Colonel René Hernández Gattorno, Lieutenant Eduardo Torres Ferrer, Brigadier General Gustavo Chui Beltrán—all retired military officers—and Oscar Oramas, who served as Cuba's ambassador to the government in neighboring Guinea-Conakry, where the PAIGC had its headquarters.

As a teenager in the early 1960s, Pina recounted, "We would hear Fidel explain to us not only why a revolution was necessary in Cuba, but why we needed to contribute to liberation struggles of other people around the world. Che Guevara spoke about helping to create 'two, three, many Vietnams,' as the Vietnamese people were waging a heroic battle against US imperialism. And Che gave us an example with his own actions.

"It was a matter of pride to be asked to go on an internationalist mission."

Pina cited his own experience. After graduating from a FAR military school at age twenty-one, he was named head of an artillery unit. That year, 1965, Che was leading a column of 130 Cuban combatants to support the liberation struggle in the Congo.

"The mission was secret," he said, "but more combatants were being recruited as reinforcements. Five additional columns were being organized to go to the Congo.

"In August I was approached by a FAR officer. He asked if I had graduated as a mortar gunner. I told him no, I had trained as a specialist in multiple rocket launchers. 'That's a shame,' he said, 'because we had an internationalist mission for you, and we need mortar gunners.'

"I didn't want to miss my chance. I told the officer, 'But I *can* do it. With the mortar training I did receive, I can do the job!' That's how I joined a group that began training to go to the Congo."

Before the end of the year, however, the Cuban mission in the Congo came to an end. "Some of us were then chosen to go to Guinea-Bissau instead," Pina said. "I was in the group that arrived in June 1966 on the ship *Lidia Doce*."

**Why Fidel chose Dreke to head mission**

Pina noted that Dreke, deputy commander under Guevara of the Congo mission, had by that time returned to Cuba and was head of the unit of the Interior Ministry training combatants, both Cubans and others, for missions abroad. At the end of 1966 Fidel Castro decided that the initial officer in charge of the Guinea-Bissau mission wasn't up to the task. Fidel sent for Dreke and told him, "You have to take charge of the mission."

Why Dreke? "I want to explain something to you," Pina said. "It's important. Fidel chose Dreke because he needed an experienced military commander, someone who had led troops in combat and demonstrated his ability to make decisions in a complex guerrilla war being fought on three fronts.

"Second, he wanted someone who was familiar with the thinking of our country's top leadership and was able to transmit that to, and work with, Guinean leaders like Cabral.

**"It's important for people, especially the new generations, to know the history of Cuba's internationalism."** —GUSTAVO CHUI BELTRÁN

COURTESY OF VÍCTOR DREKE

Northern Front, Guinea-Bissau, 1967. From left: Eduardo Torres Ferrer ("Coqui"), Alfonso Pérez Morales ("Pina"), Francisco "Chico" Mendes, and Alberto Castell Florit ("Quintín"). Mendes was a PAIGC commander; the other three were Cuban combatants. Pérez Morales was head of the unit of Cuban combatants in the north.

EDITORIAL CAPITÁN SAN LUIS

René Hernández Gattorno (sitting, with hat) and other combatants cross river from Guinea into Guinea-Bissau, 1972. Gattorno took part in decisive battles that defeated Portuguese colonial army.

PHOTO OF TORRES FERRER BY MARY-ALICE WATERS, OTHERS BY JONATHAN SILBERMAN/MILITANT

**CLOCKWISE FROM TOP LEFT:** Lt. Col. Alfonso Pérez Morales, Col. René Hernández Gattorno, Brig. Gen. Gustavo Chui Beltrán, Lt. Eduardo Torres Ferrer, all retired military officers, and former ambassador Oscar Oramas.

Pérez Morales, Gattorno, and Torres Ferrer were among the Cubans who fought in Guinea-Bissau. Chui was second-in-command of the 10th Directorate of the Revolutionary Armed Forces, which oversaw Cuba's military missions in Guinea-Bissau and other countries. Oramas was Cuba's ambassador to Guinea-Conakry during the independence war.

"And third, Fidel wanted someone who had been through the mission in the Congo. That was a bitter experience for us. And bitterness can lead to demoralization. Fidel knew we had to have a different kind of experience in Africa, and Guinea-Bissau was the place for that. The caliber of Cabral's leadership made that possible.

"Our commander in chief told Dreke to take with him the best *compañeros* who had fought with him in the Congo."

Eduardo Torres Ferrer, known by his friends and comrades as Coqui, was one of the Congo veterans who in 1966 readily accepted the new combat mission in Guinea-Bissau.

"Our experience in Guinea-Bissau was very different from the Congo," said Coqui, who during the Congo campaign Che had given the nom de guerre Nane ("eight" in Swahili).

"Like in Cuba, the commanders in Guinea-Bissau fought on the front lines alongside their men," said Coqui, who had fought in the Rebel Army during Cuba's revolutionary war. "But that wasn't the case in the Congolese movement," whose leaders lived and spent most of their time in various African and European capitals.

The Congolese movement was unable to overcome its internal leadership rivalries, lack of discipline, and reliance on tribal loyalties and superstition. Eventually its leaders decided to end the fighting, and at their request Cuba withdrew its combatants.

"The PAIGC was different," Coqui said. "It was a disciplined organization with a serious leadership. The Guinean fighters were courageous. We fought side by side with them. Our experience there really lifted the morale of compañeros who had been through the experience of the Congo."

After his initial stint in 1966–67, Coqui returned to Guinea-Bissau in 1971. And again in 1975–77, as second secretary in Cuba's embassy in the newly independent country. He later took part in two internationalist missions in Angola.

Pina vividly recalled the comradeship forged between the PAIGC fighters and Cuban internationalists. "I'll give you an example. During an attack on the Portuguese garrison in Buba in August 1966, we were with Umaro Djaló, deputy commander of the Southern Front. At one point Umaro felt an enemy rocket approaching and threw himself on top of one of our compañeros, Roberto Rodríguez. Umaro was wounded, and we had to evacuate him. He saved Roberto's life.

"That's how close we were. It felt like they were Cubans and we were Guineans."

### Amílcar fought to overcome tribalism

Amílcar Cabral's leadership was decisive to the success of the independence struggle in Guinea-Bissau and Cape Verde. "He was one of the most outstanding revolutionary leaders in Africa," said Coqui.

Pina first met Cabral soon after arriving in Conakry. "There we were taken to a PAIGC school where war orphans and other Guinean children were studying. What we heard from the children about their families—and what Amílcar explained to us about the conditions of life under Portuguese rule and the struggle they were waging—made a deep impression on us."

As head of the Cuban combatants in the Northern Front, Pina got to know Cabral. "He was a demanding leader, but very human. He knew his people."

"Amílcar forged a united movement," said René Hernández Gattorno, who first served in Guinea-Bissau in 1972 and again during the decisive months of 1973. Gattorno later played a leadership role in Cuba's combat operations in Angola, as well as internationalist missions in Congo-Brazzaville and Nicaragua.

"The guerrilla movement included fighters from all the different tribal groups—Balantas, Fulas, Manjacos, others—as well as from Cape Verde," he said. "Amílcar fought to overcome tribalism, which has done so much damage to liberation movements in many African countries. And he worked to unite Guineans and Cape Verdeans."

The PAIGC under Cabral's leadership made important advances in breaking down those obstacles, Pina noted. "Yes, there were Fula soldiers in the Portuguese colonial army. But there were also many Fulas in the liberation army—Commander Umaro Djaló was a Fula. Over the course of the struggle, PAIGC fighters stopped referring to themselves as Fula or Mandinga or Balanta or from another tribe. They would insist, 'I'm Guinean.'"

Nonetheless, the Portuguese regime never stopped probing every opportunity to foster divisions, especially between Guineans and Cape Verdeans.

"They undoubtedly used the underlying divisions to recruit a small group of PAIGC members who assassinated Amílcar on January 20, 1973," Pina noted. The conspirators, headed by Inocêncio Kani, a former PAIGC officer, were Guineans who resented the prominent role of Cape Verdeans—including Amílcar Cabral, his brother Luís Cabral, and Aristides Pereira—in the PAIGC leadership.

### Cabral's support to women's rights

One of Cabral's outstanding leadership qualities, Pina emphasized, was his efforts to integrate women into the liberation movement at all levels. "He was one of the first African leaders to promote equal rights for women," he noted.

"Women played a big role in the struggle. Many became leaders. One of the most exceptional was Titina Silá. I got to know Titina in the Northern Front. She was head of a combat unit at the time she was killed in 1973."

With Cabral's active support, women cadres like Silá stood up to antiwoman prejudices and increasingly won respect from their male fellow fighters and more broadly in Guinean society.

The importance Cabral gave to the fight for women's emancipation was part of "his overall vision of the society they were fighting to create," said Oscar Oramas, who, as Cuba's ambassador in Conakry from 1966 to 1973, worked closely with the PAIGC leader.

"In the liberated zones, Amílcar was not only preparing the Guinean people for an independent nation," Oramas said. "His goal was to begin to create conditions for a society without the exploitation they had suffered under Portuguese rule. In those areas, they built hospitals, schools, and 'people's stores.' They created village committees to administer local affairs."

"It was like a state within another state," said Coqui. "It reminded me of what the Rebel Army did in the Second Eastern Front—the beginning of a social revolution."

Coqui, born into a peasant family in Santiago de Cuba province, joined the Rebel Army in 1958 and fought in the Second Eastern Front. In that southeastern region of Cuba, freed from the Batista dictatorship's control even before the revolution's triumph, the Rebel Army under the leadership of Fidel and Raúl Castro organized workers and peasants to build schools and clinics, initiate a land reform and a literacy campaign, combat crime, administer justice, and other steps to implement the program of the revolutionary movement.

**Leadership of Commander Argüelles**

The Cuban leadership's commitment to Cabral and the independence movement in Guinea-Bissau was registered by Castro's decision, at a critical stage of the war, to send Commander Raúl Díaz Argüelles to collaborate directly with the PAIGC on the battlefield.

Gustavo Chui Beltrán told us a little about this virtually unknown chapter in the history of Cuban internationalism.

In 1972 Díaz Argüelles was named head of the newly established 10th Directorate of the Revolutionary Armed Forces (FAR), which oversaw all of Cuba's military missions abroad and trained revolutionary fighters from other Latin American and African countries. Chui was the Directorate's second-in-command; he became its head in 1975, after Argüelles fell in combat in Angola. In that responsibility he worked closely with both Fidel Castro and Raúl Castro, head of the FAR.

"Fidel sent Argüelles to Guinea-Bissau to assess the situation and meet with Amílcar and other PAIGC leaders," said Chui. "I was responsible for sending a group of seasoned FAR officers to accompany Argüelles, officers like Colonel Wilfredo Colás ("Patifino") and Colonel René Hernández Gattorno who took part in some of the subsequent battles there." Over the course of several visits in 1972, "Argüelles traveled through the liberated territories. He saw that the Portuguese forces had been dealt serious blows, and it was now important to launch an offensive that could defeat the Portuguese colonial army."

The Portuguese, having lost control of the majority of Guinean territory, no longer ventured out of their bases, relying more and more on deadly aerial attacks. To minimize losses the PAIGC leadership was waging a war of attrition, together with a political campaign that was gaining broad international support. Cabral expected that Lisbon, faced with growing worldwide pressure, could eventually be forced into negotiations to grant independence.

"With Fidel's support, Argüelles talked with Cabral and argued that now was the time to take the initiative and start attacking and taking enemy garrisons," Chui said. Otherwise, the morale of the combatants would suffer.

By the end of that year Cabral became convinced of the Cuban proposal, but he was assassinated before it could be carried out.

"After Amílcar's death, Fidel instructed Argüelles to return to Guinea-Bissau to meet with Aristides Pereira, Nino [João Bernardo Vieira], and other PAIGC leaders," Chui said. "They agreed with the Cuban proposal to launch an offensive."

In the meantime, the PAIGC had finally begun to receive shoulder-launched antiaircraft weapons from the Soviet government, which Cabral had requested months earlier. These missiles—called *Strela* (arrow) in Russian and *Flecha* in Spanish—gave the liberation fighters effective protection from Portuguese air attacks.

After some weeks of training to use the Flechas, PAIGC combatants, assisted by the Cuban antiaircraft artillery instructors, began shooting down one enemy plane after another. Within the first two weeks they had downed ten aircraft, including one piloted by an air force commander who was killed in the crash. The Portuguese soon stopped sending their demoralized pilots on low-flying combat missions.

The PAIGC, Chui said, "then launched a campaign called 'Operation Amílcar Cabral.' It was jointly directed by Commanders Nino and Argüelles."

The successful operation, Chui noted, "gave a big boost to the PAIGC fighters," whose morale had suffered after Cabral's assassination.

### Decisive battle of Guiledje

Operation Amílcar Cabral included attacks on Portuguese garrisons in the north and the south, but its focal point was the May 1973 battle of Guiledje. Gattorno, who was part of it, told us how the events unfolded.

Guiledje was a large fortified garrison in the south, near the border with Guinea-Conakry. Its main responsibility was to prevent the guerrillas from being resupplied across the border. From the PAIGC command post, "Commander Argüelles instructed us to capture the garrison," Gattorno said. The rebel force included hundreds of PAIGC fighters and a group of Cuban combatants.

On May 18 a PAIGC-Cuban unit ambushed a Portuguese reconnaissance patrol on the supply road between Guiledje and the nearby Gadamael garrison. Then other fighters, from positions hidden in the jungle several miles away, launched a massive artillery assault on the Guiledje base. "The Portuguese planes, flying high, couldn't spot them," Gattorno said.

The combatants hammered the Guiledje base with heavy mortar and cannon fire. After several days, the artillery response from the Portuguese fort stopped.

"On May 25 Argüelles told me to lead a unit of combatants to the garrison," Gattorno said. "We confirmed the Portuguese had withdrawn."

The victory at Guiledje was the turning point that hastened the end of the war.

"When we entered the garrison we found an enormous amount of military hardware and food supplies left behind," Gattorno said. "The only ones still there were some of the Fula villagers.

"To protect themselves, the colonialists had made the local population live in huts inside the perimeter of that large garrison. There were underground shelters, but the villagers weren't allowed to use them—they were only for the soldiers. Many civilians died in the battle.

"We were witnesses to how the Portuguese imperialists used Guineans—Fulas who were supposedly their allies—as human shields. It's important for the world to know about that crime. The imperialists have used civilians as human shields in many parts of the world."

Gattorno recalled that in 2010, he and other Cuban veterans of the Guinea-Bissau war were invited back to an event commemorating the liberation struggle. "Our hosts took us to Guiledje. Now there is a museum of independence where the barracks once stood.

"I remember a skinny guy working at the museum who pointed out something about the former garrison. I asked him, 'Were you one of the fighters who went in with me?'

"He said, 'No, I was living here with my family. They were all killed,'" Gattorno told us with visible emotion. "Afterward I learned that this man is devoted to the work of the museum, a real patriot."

Gattorno added that during his time on the battle front he also saw some of the captured Portuguese soldiers. "The imperialists used them as cannon fodder too. Those young men were sons of poor peasants. Their hands were calloused. Many were illiterate," said Gattorno, who himself grew up in a sugar mill town in central Cuba.

"When we captured Portuguese soldiers, we didn't detain them. They moved freely in the guerrilla camp, fetching us water and firewood. They would tell us, 'We don't want to return to the army. Please turn me over to the Red Cross.' And that's what the PAIGC did."

Oramas noted that in his discussions with Cabral, "He always insisted that the enemy of the Guinean and Cape Verdean people was the colonial regime, not the Portuguese people. Amílcar had lived and studied in Portugal and had seen the poverty in which many people lived. The PAIGC appealed to the soldiers. That approach hastened the defeat of the Portuguese army."

**Guinea-Bissau: detonator of Portuguese revolution**

Lisbon's defeat in Guinea-Bissau and Cape Verde had worldwide repercussions. "But many historical accounts omit or minimize the importance of that victory," said Chui.

"Guinea-Bissau is a small country. But it was there that the Portuguese army became bogged down and demoralized by the advances of the anticolonial struggle. In 1973 and 1974 they suffered crushing defeats at the hands of the PAIGC guerrillas—cadres who had been forged under the leadership of Amílcar Cabral."

Chui noted that the fascist regime in Portugal, which had been in power since the 1930s, "had become weakened by the popular discontent over its brutal dictatorship and the economic ruin of the country.

"What detonated the fall of the regime was its defeat in Guinea-Bissau."

**“Our enemy isn’t the people of Portugal. Our enemy is Portuguese colonialism.”** —AMÍLCAR CABRAL, 1965

FMSMB/CASA COMUM-AMÍLCAR CABRAL

Guerrilla fighters play soccer match with captured Portuguese soldiers during independence war.

Most soldiers “were sons of poor peasants. Their hands were calloused; many were illiterate,” said Cuban combatant René Hernández Gattorno, who fought alongside the PAIGC. “The Portuguese imperialists used these young men as cannon fodder.”

The prisoners of war—who included growing numbers of army deserters—were treated with dignity. They were often allowed to share tasks such as collecting firewood and carrying water. The liberation fighters would turn them over to the Red Cross when the opportunity arose, not to the Portuguese army.

Many of the young officers who had been sent to fight in the colonial war, Chui said, "took part in the military coup that overthrew the dictatorship on April 25, 1974—what became known as the Carnation Revolution." That sparked a revolutionary upsurge by millions of workers, peasants, and students in Portugal.

"These events in turn led to the collapse of the Portuguese colonial empire. To the independence not only of Guinea-Bissau and Cape Verde but of Mozambique, São Tomé and Príncipe, and Angola."

A decade and a half later, "the defeat of the invading South African army in Angola led to the end of the apartheid regime and the independence of Namibia," said Chui, who led combat units in Cuba's internationalist combat mission in Angola in 1986–88 and was severely wounded.

"The significance of the victory in Guinea-Bissau and Cape Verde, and the contribution that Cuban internationalists made to it, are not well known," Chui said.

"But it's important, especially for the new generations, to know this history."

"Those not willing to fight for the freedom of others will never be able to fight for their own," Dreke concluded, citing the words of truth Fidel spoke to the Cuban people, as they mobilized to support their Angolan and Namibian brothers and sisters.

"And Fidel was right," Dreke said. "Our participation in the liberation struggles in Africa and other parts of the world made the Cuban people stronger. Those actions reinforced the values of our socialist revolution that we continue to defend today."

# TIMELINE

**1462** – Portuguese monarchy establishes settlement in the Cape Verde island chain. Over four centuries the islands, populated by Africans brought from the Guinean coast and forced into slavery, become Portuguese center for transatlantic slave trade.

**1687** – Bissau founded as Portuguese trading post.

**1869** – Slavery banned in Portuguese territories.

**1878** – Facing fierce resistance by peoples of Guinea, Lisbon launches "pacification" wars, gains full control only by 1936.

**1885** – At Berlin Conference, European imperialist powers carve up most of Africa among themselves. They formally recognize borders of "Portuguese" Guinea.

**1933** – Fascist regime consolidated in Portugal, headed by António Salazar.

**1940s** – Severe droughts in Cape Verde. Lisbon does nothing to alleviate conditions; famine kills 45,000, a quarter of the population.

**1945–52** – Amílcar Cabral studies at University of Lisbon, becomes involved in political activity. He works with other African students—from Angola, Cape Verde, Mozambique, and São Tomé—who come to know each other. Several later become leaders of anticolonial struggles in their countries.

**1953 February 3** – Batepá massacre in São Tomé. Colonial forces kill hundreds of workers resisting forced labor on cacao plantations, sparking outrage among Africans throughout Portugal's colonies.

**1954** – Start of Algerian independence war against French rule.

**1956 September 19** – Cabral and five others meet clandestinely in Bissau to found African Party for the Independence of Guinea and Cape Verde (PAIGC). In late 1950s, party members help lead trade union and political struggles.

**July–December** – Gamal Abdel Nasser government in Egypt nationalizes imperialist-owned Suez Canal; British, French, Israeli governments invade. Washington, pursuing its own rival interests in region, helps Egypt restore its sovereignty over canal.

**December 10** – Founding of Popular Movement for the Liberation of Angola (MPLA), led by Agostinho Neto. Cabral takes part in founding.

**1957** – Ghana wins independence from British rule. Kwame Nkrumah elected first president.

**1958** – As anticolonial activity spreads, Paris holds referendums in African colonies on whether to remain part of France. Ahmed Sékou Touré leads successful campaign for "No" vote in Guinea-Conakry, which becomes independent. Sékou Touré elected president.

**1959 January 1** – Revolutionary victory in Cuba. After Rebel Army led by Fidel Castro takes major cities of Santiago de Cuba and Santa Clara, Batista dictatorship falls. Working people respond to call for popular insurrection and general strike, bring revolutionary government to power.

**August 3** – Strike by port workers and riverboat sailors in Bissau. Portuguese troops kill 50 on Pidjiguiti docks. Afterward, PAIGC shifts strategy, prepares for a guerrilla war to win independence. Newly independent Guinea-Conakry agrees to become rear base.

**1960–62** – PAIGC sends cadres to villages across countryside to win confidence of and organize population. Movement recruits from all tribal groups.

**1960** – As anti-imperialist struggles spread worldwide, 17 more African countries gain independence.

**1961 January 17** – Patrice Lumumba, prime minister of newly independent Congo, murdered by US- and Belgian-backed Congolese forces.

**February 4** – Popular Movement for the Liberation of Angola (MPLA), led by Agostinho Neto, launches independence war against Portuguese rule with attack on colonial police in Luanda.

**March 15** – Holden Roberto's National Front for the Liberation of Angola, FNLA (then the Union of African Peoples), an MPLA rival based on Bakongo tribe, launches armed campaign against Portugal in northern Angola. They slaughter 1,000 Portuguese settlers and 6,000 migrant workers of the Ovimbundu tribe laboring on coffee plantations. Portuguese army responds destroying dozens of villages and killing 20,000 Africans. In subsequent years, FNLA is covertly backed by Washington and South African apartheid regime.

**April 17–19** – US-organized mercenary invasion of Cuba is defeated by revolutionary militias and armed forces at Bay of Pigs.

**December** – Cuba sends arms to Algerian independence fighters, brings back to Cuba war orphans needing medical treatment.

**1962 February** – Washington expands its economic war on Cuban Revolution, imposing ban on most US trade with and travel to the island.

**February 4** – One million Cubans gather in Plaza of the Revolution, ratify Second Declaration of Havana, which points to Cuba's socialist revolution as the way forward for working people throughout the Americas.

**July 5** – Algeria wins independence from France after eight-year war.

**October 22–28** – As Kennedy administration brings world to brink of nuclear conflict in "missile crisis," Cuban workers and farmers mobilize to deter US invasion.

**1963 January 23** – PAIGC attacks Tite barracks in southern Guinea-Bissau, launching guerrilla war against Portuguese rule.

**April–May** – Black rights fighters in Birmingham, Alabama mobilize to resist police assaults. "Battle of Birmingham" is turning point in working-class-led movement that brings down Jim Crow racial segregation in US South—a movement strengthened by deepening liberation struggles in Africa.

**May** – Team of volunteer doctors and nurses goes to Algeria, in Cuban Revolution's first internationalist medical mission.

**October** – Nearly 700 Cuban combatants help Algeria deter US-backed Moroccan invasion.

**1964 January–March** – On island of Como, PAIGC fighters and Balanta rice farmers, men and women, beat back 75-day-long assault by 3,000 Portuguese troops, the rebels' first major military victory.

**February** – PAIGC holds first congress in Cassacá. Cabral leads political battle to defeat PAIGC leaders who act like local warlords, abusing women and killing villagers they accuse of "witchcraft."

**April–November** – Malcolm X makes two trips through Africa and Mideast, meeting revolutionaries and heads of state as well as speaking to popular audiences.

**September 25** – FRELIMO (Mozambique Liberation Front) launches war against Portuguese colonial rule.

**December** – Ernesto Che Guevara begins three-month trip to eight African countries, meets leaders of governments and liberation movements, including Amílcar Cabral.

**1965 April–November** – Column of 130 Cuban volunteers under Guevara's leadership, with Víctor Dreke as second-in-command, joins supporters of Lumumba in Congo fighting pro-imperialist Mobutu regime.

**1966 January** – Cabral speaks at Tricontinental Conference in Havana. Spends three days traveling through Escambray Mountains with Fidel Castro, who pledges aid to Guinea-Bissau independence struggle.

**May–June** – First Cuban artillery instructors arrive in Guinea-Bissau.

**October** – Cubans start training MPLA combatants in Congo-Brazzaville for independence war in Angola.

**1967 February** – Dreke heads Cuban military mission in Guinea-Bissau and Guinea-Conakry. He completes mission and returns to Cuba in late 1968.

**October** – Che Guevara, wounded in Bolivia, is murdered by agents acting for US and Bolivian governments. In his honor, Cabral announces guerrilla campaign in Guinea-Bissau called Operation "Che will not die."

**1968 September** – Portuguese dictator António Salazar suffers stroke, is replaced by Marcelo Caetano.

**1970 November 22** – Lisbon-organized commando raid on Conakry, seeking to overthrow Sékou Touré government and deal blow to PAIGC, is defeated by loyal troops and Cuban-trained militias.

**1971 December** – Cuban leadership sends Commander Raúl Díaz Argüelles on first of several trips to Guinea-Bissau to collaborate with PAIGC leaders in liberation war.

**1972 May 3–8** – Fidel Castro tours Guinea with President Sékou Touré. Meets with Amílcar Cabral and Aristides Pereira in Conakry.

**1973 January 20** – Cabral assassinated in Conakry by a group, headed by Inocêncio Kani, of disaffected PAIGC members organized by Portuguese secret police. PAIGC chooses Aristides Pereira to replace Cabral as general secretary.

**March 23** – PAIGC artillery gunners, supervised by Cuban instructors, begin to shoot down Portuguese planes with newly acquired Flecha surface-to-air missiles.

**May 17** – PAIGC launches "Operation Amílcar Cabral," led by commanders João Bernardo "Nino" Vieira and Raúl Díaz Argüelles.

**May 25** – Rebel forces take Guiledje fortified base in the south, a turning point in the war. Over subsequent months Portuguese troops abandon other key garrisons.

**July** – Thousands in London protest Caetano's visit and condemn December 1972 massacre of 400 villagers in Wiriyamu, Mozambique by Portuguese soldiers.

**September 24** – In Madina do Boé, southern Guinea-Bissau, PAIGC holds National Popular Assembly; 120 representatives elected by population in liberated areas proclaim independent state and elect Luís Cabral president. New republic is recognized by 80 countries and admitted to Organization of African Unity.

**1974** – **February 12** – Copa garrison, encircled for weeks, falls to PAIGC; before the attack, rebel forces silently evacuate the surrounding civilian population and their cattle. Independence struggle intensifies in cities and towns.

**April 25** – PAIGC victories in Guinea-Bissau precipitate crisis in Portuguese regime. Military coup in Lisbon overthrows Caetano dictatorship, setting off mass revolutionary upsurge known as Carnation Revolution.

**September 10** – Lisbon recognizes Guinea-Bissau's independence.

**September 12** – Haile Selassie monarchy overthrown in Ethiopia. Land reform and other antifeudal measures by new government, backed by peasant and worker mobilizations.

**1975 April 30** – As US forces abandon Saigon (Ho Chi Minh City), Vietnamese fighters win decades-long battle for liberation and national reunification.

**June 25** – Mozambique wins independence from Portuguese rule. Samora Machel of FRELIMO, which led the struggle, becomes president.

**July 5** – In Cape Verde months of rising mass protests including a general strike culminate with country's independence. Aristides Pereira is elected first president.

**July 12** – São Tomé wins independence from Portuguese rule.

**October 14** – As independence of Angola approaches, South African troops invade it from south; Zaire (Congo) troops and other US-backed forces invade from north in attempt to prevent MPLA from forming government.

**November 5** – In response to Angolan government request Cuban leadership sends volunteer combatants to help repel invaders.

**November 11** – Angola declares independence. MPLA leader Agostinho Neto is first president.

**1976 March 27** – Angolan and Cuban combatants drive last of invading South African troops out of Angola. Over 16 years, 425,000 Cuban volunteers serve in Angola to help defeat two more South African invasions.

**1986** – Cuban medical mission establishes Raúl Díaz Argüelles School of Medicine in Guinea-Bissau.

**1988 March** – Cuban and Angolan combatants defeat South African assault at Cuito Cuanavale, leading to complete withdrawal of Pretoria's troops from Angola.

**1990 February 11** – In face of rising struggles in South Africa, Nelson Mandela, leader of African National Congress, is released from prison after 27 years.

**March 21** – Namibia declares independence.

**1994 April 27** – Mandela is elected president of South Africa in first post-apartheid election.

**2014–15** – Cuban medical volunteers help end deadly Ebola epidemic in Liberia, Sierra Leone, and Guinea-Conakry.

# INDEX

# CUBA'S SOCIALIST REVOLUTION

*New!*

**Revolution and the Road to Peace in Colombia**

The Example of the Cuban Revolution

FIDEL CASTRO

"No crime can be committed in the name of revolution," Fidel Castro declares, drawing from the example set by working people of Cuba as they took state power out of the hands of its capitalist rulers. In 2008, as part of efforts to end six decades of armed conflict in Colombia, he shared the exemplary record of Cuba's revolutionary struggle with the Revolutionary Armed Forces of Colombia (FARC) and the world. $10. Also in Spanish and French.

## Women in Cuba: The Making of a Revolution Within the Revolution

VILMA ESPÍN, ASELA DE LOS SANTOS
YOLANDA FERRER

The integration of women in the ranks and leadership of the Cuban Revolution was intertwined with the proletarian course led by Fidel Castro from the start. This is the story of that revolution and how it transformed the women and men who made it. $17. Also in Spanish, Farsi, Greek.

## The First and Second Declarations of Havana

Nowhere are the questions of revolutionary strategy that today confront men and women on the front lines of struggles in the Americas addressed with greater truthfulness and clarity than in these uncompromising indictments of imperialist plunder and "the exploitation of man by man." Adopted by million-strong assemblies of the Cuban people in 1960 and 1962. $10. Also in Spanish, French, Farsi, Arabic, Greek.

# Cuba's internationalist

## FROM THE ESCAMBRAY TO THE CONGO

In the Whirlwind of the Cuban Revolution

VÍCTOR DREKE

A lifelong revolutionary leader describes his experiences in the battles by working people that led Cuba to become the first Free Territory of the Americas. In the defeat of US-backed counterrevolutionaries in Cuba's Escambray mountains. And in Cuba's internationalist combat missions in the Congo in 1965 under Che Guevara's command, and in Guinea-Bissau's independence war against Portuguese rule. $15. Also in Spanish.

## THE BOLIVIAN DIARY OF ERNESTO CHE GUEVARA

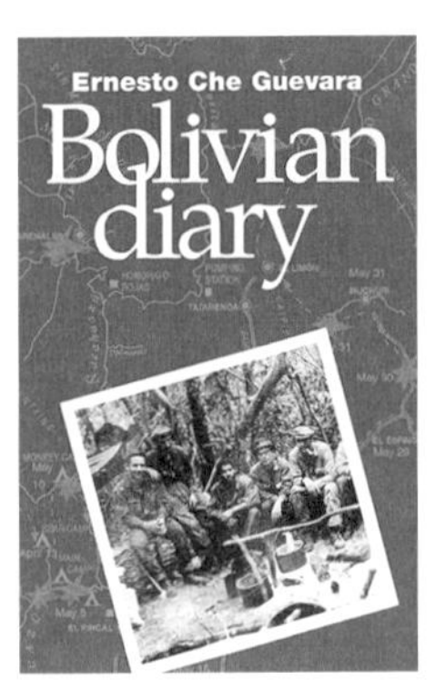


Guevara's day-by-day chronicle of the 1966–67 guerrilla campaign in Bolivia, an effort to forge a continent-wide revolutionary movement of workers and peasants and open the road to socialist revolution in South America. $23. Also in Spanish.

## CAPITALISM AND THE TRANSFORMATION OF AFRICA

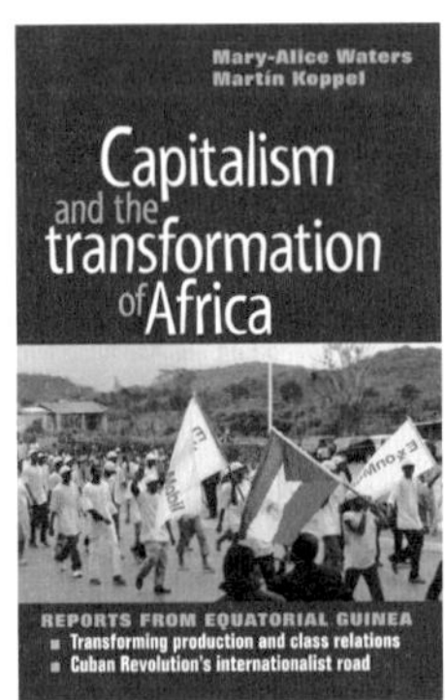


Reports from Equatorial Guinea

MARY-ALICE WATERS, MARTÍN KOPPEL

Describes how, as Equatorial Guinea is pulled into the world market, both a capitalist class and a working class are being born. And documents the work of volunteer Cuban health-care workers there—an expression of the living example of Cuba's socialist revolution. $10. Also in Spanish and Farsi.

# solidarity

## CUBA AND ANGOLA

The War for Freedom

HARRY VILLEGAS ("POMBO")

The story of Cuba's unparalleled contribution to the fight to free Africa from the scourge of apartheid. And how, in the doing, Cuba's socialist revolution was strengthened. $10. Also in Spanish, Farsi, Greek.

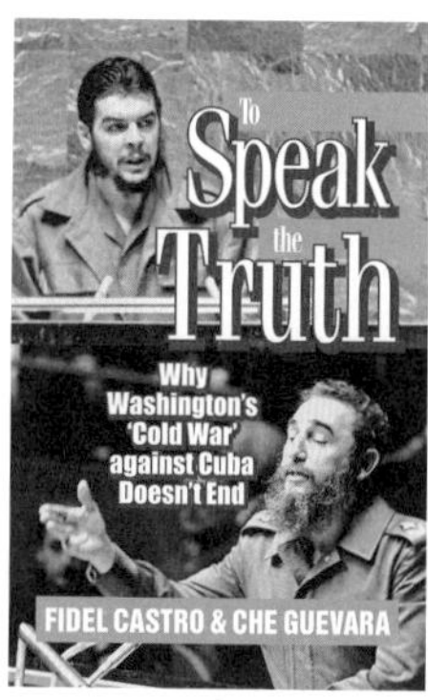


## TO SPEAK THE TRUTH

Why Washington's 'Cold War' Against Cuba Doesn't End

FIDEL CASTRO, CHE GUEVARA

In historic speeches before the United Nations and UN bodies, Guevara and Castro address the peoples of the world, explaining why the US government so fears the example set by the socialist revolution in Cuba. $15. Also in Greek.

## RED ZONE

Cuba and the Battle against Ebola in West Africa

ENRIQUE UBIETA GÓMEZ

In 2014 West Africa was hit by the largest recorded Ebola epidemic. Answering a global call, Cuba's revolutionary socialist government provided what no other country even tried to—more than 200 volunteer doctors and nurses. "The heroic actions of Cuba's army of white coats occupies a place of honor in history," said Cuban leader Fidel Castro. $17. Also in Spanish.

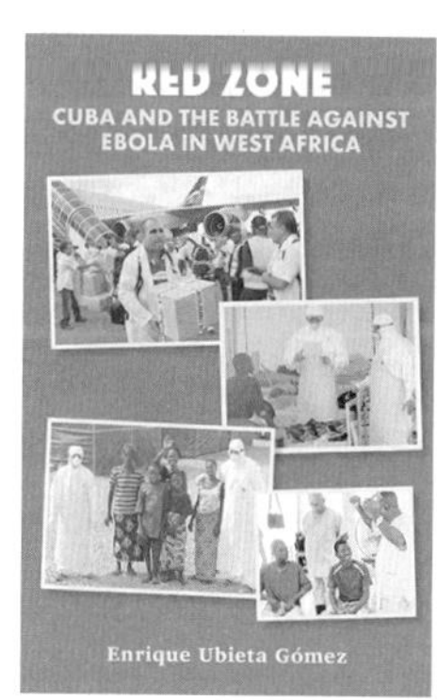

# CAPITALIST CRISIS AND THE FIGHT FOR WORKERS POWER

## Are They Rich Because They're Smart?

Class, Privilege, and Learning Under Capitalism

JACK BARNES

Exposes growing class inequalities in the US and the self-serving rationalizations of well-paid professionals who think their "brilliance" equips them to "regulate" working people, who don't know what's in our own best interest. $10. Also in Spanish, French, Farsi, Arabic, Greek.

## Cuba and the Coming American Revolution

JACK BARNES

This is a book about the example set by the Cuban people that socialist revolution is not only necessary—it can be made. A book about the struggles of workers and other exploited producers in the imperialist heartland, and the youth attracted to them. About the class struggle in the US, where the revolutionary capacities of working people are as utterly discounted by the ruling powers as were those of the Cuban toilers. $10. Also in Spanish, French, Farsi.

## The Low Point of Labor Resistance Is Behind Us

The Socialist Workers Party Looks Forward

JACK BARNES, MARY-ALICE WATERS, STEVE CLARK

The global order imposed by Washington is shattering. A long retreat by the working class and unions has come to an end. The bosses and their government are stepping up attacks on our wages, conditions, and constitutional rights. This book highlights opportunities for building a mass proletarian party able to lead the struggle to end capitalist rule, opening a socialist future for humanity. $10. Also in Spanish, French, Greek.

## Malcolm X, Black Liberation, and the Road to Workers Power

JACK BARNES

"The conquest of state power by a class-conscious vanguard of the working class is the mightiest weapon possible in the fight against Black oppression, the subjugation of women, Jew-hatred, and every form of human degradation inherited from class society." $20. Also in Spanish, French, Farsi, Arabic, Greek.

## Is Socialist Revolution in the US Possible?

A Necessary Debate Among Working People

MARY-ALICE WATERS

Fighting for a society only working people can create, it is our own capacities we will discover. And we will answer the question posed here with a resounding "Yes." Revolution is possible but not inevitable. That depends on us. $7. Also in Spanish, French, Farsi.

## The Fight Against Jew-Hatred and Pogroms in the Imperialist Epoch

Stakes for the International Working Class

V.I. LENIN, LEON TROTSKY
FARRELL DOBBS, JAMES P. CANNON
JACK BARNES, DAVE PRINCE

Jew-hatred and pogroms—such as Hamas carried out on October 7, 2023—are part of the social convulsions and wars of the imperialist epoch. The authors explain why fighting Jew-hatred is decisive to the working class and oppressed nations of the world—and *what is to be done to end it*. $10. Also in Spanish, French, Greek.

# BUILDING A REVOLUTIONARY WORKERS PARTY

## In Defense of Marxism

Against the Petty-Bourgeois Opposition in the Socialist Workers Party

LEON TROTSKY

A reply to those in the revolutionary workers movement in the late 1930s who buckled to bourgeois patriotism during Washington's buildup to enter World War II. Trotsky explains why only a party fighting to bring workers into its ranks and leadership can steer a communist course. In the process, he defends the materialist and dialectical foundations of Marxism. $17. Also in Spanish, French, Farsi.

## The Struggle for a Proletarian Party

JAMES P. CANNON

"The workers of America have power enough to topple the structure of capitalism at home and to lift the whole world with them when they rise," Cannon asserts. On the eve of World War II, a founder of the communist movement in the US and a leader of the Communist International in Lenin's time defends the program and party-building norms of Bolshevism. $20. Also in Spanish and Farsi.

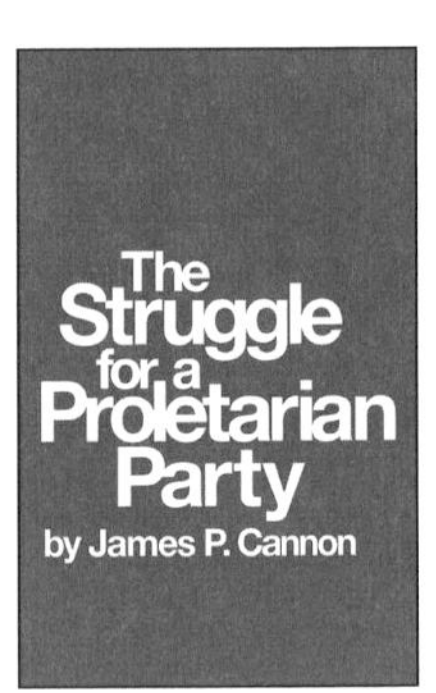


## The Founding of the Socialist Workers Party

Minutes and Resolutions, 1938–39

JAMES P. CANNON

At founding gatherings of the Socialist Workers Party in 1938–39, revolutionists in the US codified two decades of experience in building a communist party. They charted a working-class course in resisting the coming imperialist war, fighting fascism and Jew-hatred, the struggle for Black rights, forging an alliance with exploited farmers, and the battle to transform the unions into revolutionary instruments of struggle by working people. $23

## Lenin's Final Fight

Speeches and Writings, 1922–23

V.I. LENIN

In 1922 and 1923, V.I. Lenin, central leader of the world's first socialist revolution, waged what was to be his last political battle—one that was lost after his death. At stake was whether that revolutionary government and the world communist movement it led would remain on the revolutionary proletarian course that brought workers and peasants to power in Russia in 1917. $17. Also in Spanish, Farsi, Greek.

## The First Ten Years of American Communism

Report of a Participant

JAMES P. CANNON

"Stalinism has worked mightily to obliterate the honorable record of American communism in its pioneer days. Yet the Communist Party wrote such a chapter, and the young militants of the new generation ought to know about it and claim it for their own. It belongs to them."
—James P. Cannon, 1962. $17

## Socialism on Trial

Testimony at Minneapolis Sedition Trial

JAMES P. CANNON

The revolutionary program of the working class presented in federal court in 1941 on the eve of US entry into World War II. The frame-up charges of "seditious conspiracy" targeted leaders of the Socialist Workers Party. $15. Also in Spanish, French, Farsi.

# MARXIST LEADERSHIP IN THE UNITED STATES

## The Teamster Series

FARRELL DOBBS

Four books on the 1930s strikes, organizing drives, and political campaigns that transformed the Teamsters into a militant industrial union movement. Written by the organizer of these battles and leader of the Socialist Workers Party. A tool for workers seeking to use union power and advance the fight for a party of labor. $16 each, series $50. Also in Spanish. *Teamster Rebellion* is also available in French, Farsi, Greek.

## The Turn to Industry

Forging a Proletarian Party

JACK BARNES

A book about the working-class program, composition, and course of the only kind of party in the imperialist epoch worthy of the name "revolutionary." A party that can recognize the most revolutionary fact of this epoch—the worth of working people, and our capacity to change society when we organize and act to win power from the capitalist class. $15. Also in Spanish, French, Farsi, Greek.

## America's Revolutionary Heritage

Marxist Essays

GEORGE NOVACK

A materialist explanation of the American Revolution, Civil War and Radical Reconstruction, genocide against the Indians, rise of American imperialism, first wave of the fight for women's rights, and more. $23

## Revolutionary Continuity

Marxist Leadership in the U.S.

*The Early Years, 1848–1917*

*Birth of the Communist Movement, 1918–1922*

FARRELL DOBBS

"Successive generations of proletarian revolutionists have participated in the movements of the working class and its allies. . . . Marxists today owe them not only homage for their deeds. We also have a duty to learn what they did wrong as well as right so their errors are not repeated." —*Farrell Dobbs.* Two volumes, $17 each.

## Fighting Racism in World War II

FROM THE PAGES OF THE *MILITANT*

An account of struggles against racist discrimination in US war industries, the armed forces, and society as a whole from 1939 to 1945, taken from the pages of the socialist newsweekly, the *Militant*. These struggles helped lay the basis for the proletarian-based civil rights movement that followed. $20

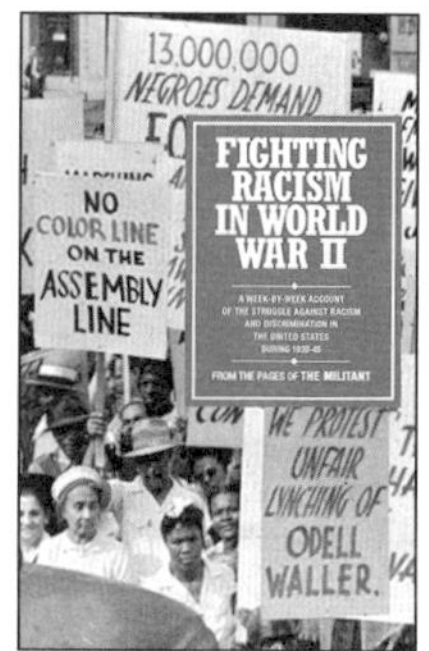


## Malcolm X Talks to Young People

Four talks and an interview given to young people in Ghana, the United Kingdom, and the United States in the last months of Malcolm's life. He discusses imperialist intervention in the Congo and Vietnam, why he stopped using the description "Black nationalism," and more. Concludes with memorial tributes by a young socialist leader to this great revolutionary. $12. Also in Spanish, French, Farsi, Greek.

# ORIGINS OF WOMEN'S OPPRESSION AND THE FIGHT TO END IT

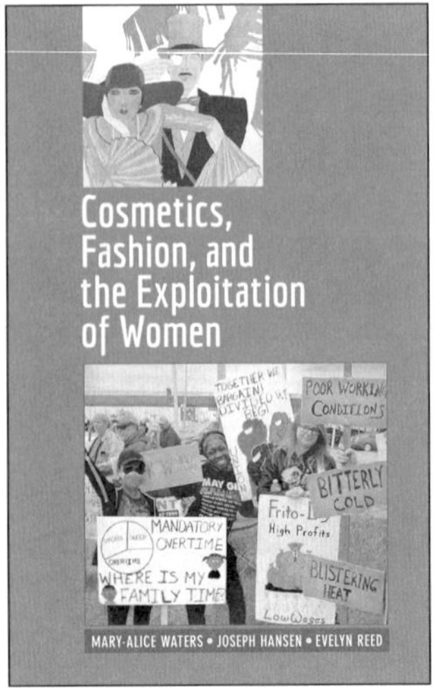


*New Expanded Edition!*

## Cosmetics, Fashion, and the Exploitation of Women

MARY-ALICE WATERS
JOSEPH HANSEN, EVELYN REED

"Norms of beauty and fashion are inseparable from the class struggle." That's the title of the opening chapter of this new edition of a lively 1950s debate in the *Militant,* a socialist newsweekly. How cosmetics and fashion monopolies rake in profits from social insecurities of women and adolescents. Why women's integration into the workforce and unions is a major advance in the fight for emancipation. A Marxist classic on the origins of women's oppression and the working-class road forward. $15. Also in Spanish, French, Farsi, Greek.

## Women's Liberation and the African Freedom Struggle

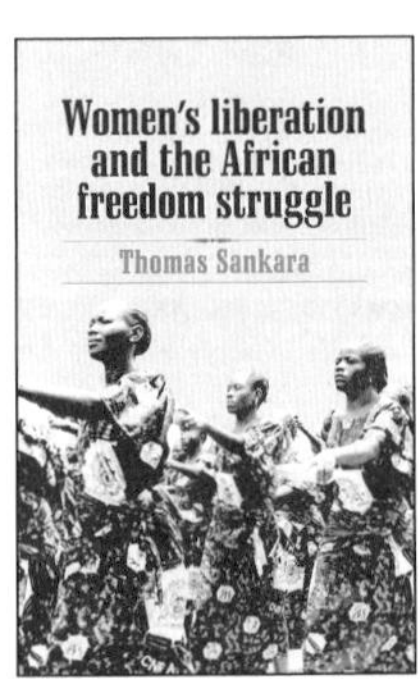


THOMAS SANKARA

"There is no true social revolution without the liberation of women," explains the leader of the 1983–87 revolution in the West African country of Burkina Faso. $5. Also in Spanish, French, Farsi.

## Capital

KARL MARX

Marx explains the workings of the capitalist system and how it produces the insoluble contradictions—including the oppression of women—that breed class struggle. He demonstrates the inevitability of the revolutionary transformation of society into one ruled for the first time by the producing majority, the working class. Three volumes, $18 each. Also in Spanish. Volume 1 available in French.

# THE LONG VIEW OF HISTORY

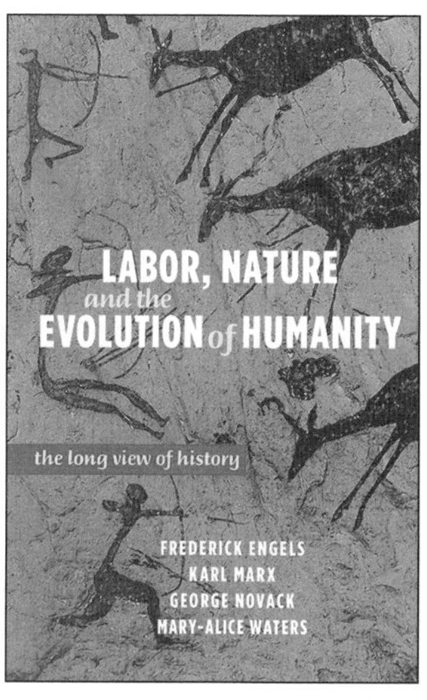


## Labor, Nature, and the Evolution of Humanity

The Long View of History

FREDERICK ENGELS, KARL MARX
GEORGE NOVACK
MARY-ALICE WATERS

Without understanding that social labor, transforming nature, has driven humanity's evolution for millions of years, working people are unable to see beyond the capitalist epoch of class exploitation that warps all human relations, ideas, and values. $12. Also in Spanish and French.

## The Communist Manifesto

KARL MARX AND FREDERICK ENGELS

Communism, say the founding leaders of the revolutionary workers movement, is not a set of ideas or preconceived "principles" but workers' line of march to power. It springs from a "movement going on under our very eyes." $5. Also in Spanish, French, Farsi, Arabic.

Pathfinder Press **accessible e-books** for the blind, those with low vision, or other challenges reading print books

For a list of current accessible titles, go to: pathfinderpress.com/collections/books-for-the-blind.

Visit bookshare.org for information on how to sign up.